EMPLOYER SECRETS

And
How to Use Them to Get the
Job and Pay YOU Want!

Phil Baker

First Edition

DreamCatcher Publishing, Inc. Florissant, Missouri

Employer Secrets
And How to Use Them to Get the Job and Pay You Want
by Phil Baker

Copyright © 2005 by DreamCatcher Publishing, Inc.

1050 St. Francois Florissant, MO 63031
Published by: DreamCatcher Publishing, Inc. Phone 314 972-1505

Printed in the United States of America
Paperback ISBN 0-9755925-0-5
Library of Congress Control Number: 2004095052

Library of Congress Cataloging-in-Publication Data
Baker, Phil, 1957-
   Employer secrets : and how to use them to get the job and pay you want! / Phil Baker.
   p. cm.
   Includes bibliographical references and index.
   LCCN 2004095052
   ISBN 0-9755925-0-5

   1. Job hunting. I. Title.

HF5382.7.B35 2005   650.14
                      QBI04-200342

This book is dedicated to you, the reader.
I hope the information within these pages
inspires and empowers you to fulfill your dreams.

Disclaimer

This book is intended to provide information on job hunting, interviewing, and negotiation. The publisher and author offer no legal or professional advice.

If legal or other advice is required the author and publisher recommend consulting the services of such.

The author and publisher of this book disclaim any liability arising from the use or application of the contents of this book.

All efforts have been made to be complete and accurate in the writing of this book. Typographical and content errors are possible, and the information herein is not to be relied upon as the only source of such information.

The buyer of this book hereby releases the author and publisher from any liability whatsoever from any reliance upon the information in this book. The buyer may return this book to the publisher in original condition with proof or purchase by receipt within ten consecutive days of purchase date for a refund if the buyer does not wish to be fully bound by all of the statements above.

Some of the names of people in this book have been changed. Statements in this book referring to the actions of people or employers, singular or plural, do not describe the actions of all employers or any specific employers, companies, or people.

Any references herein to additional information from the website www.employersecrets.com were made at the time of printing and are strictly for reference as additional publications and information from the website or other sources might not be available or free.

Acknowledgements

Corneas come from organ donors that have passed. As donors remain anonymous, I would like to take this opportunity to say thank you to everyone who has been an organ donor. As a recipient I have experienced the bestowed inspiration brought on by this selfless act. For those who have grieved over the loss of such a person, I would like to tell you that your loved ones made contributions that do live on. Without the ultimate generosity of an anonymous one in particular, this book would not have been written. Thank you.

Thank you to my children, your phone calls and taps upon my shoulder while I wrote this book kept me from missing some of life's greatest moments.

Thank you to Ramon and Kathy Baker for your review and important contributions.

Stephen Gruszka is a positive man who will go far and has provided me business and moral support above and beyond the call of duty.

Sharon Peterman, whose work ethic and kindness deserve recognition beyond earthly reward.

Dr. Jay Pepose, for his elaborate skill so rarely coupled with genuine humility.

Thank you Mr. Rinehart. I think that without a simple act of generosity I would not have been as inspired to push so hard and could have missed many new insights altogether.

Thank you to the late Walter Bush, whose acts of personal encouragement survive.

TABLE OF CONTENTS

I. Employers, Secrets, and YOU

1. How I Discovered Employer Secrets

One day I was sitting in seventh grade math class, looking at the United States Flag hanging flat on the wall at the front of our room. I must have been bored because I remember trying to count the stars on the flag. I couldn't do it! That discovery was the beginning of a physical aberration that changed my life forever. I was thirteen years old, and this was the first time I had blurry vision.

My mother took me to an eye doctor who diagnosed me with 'case of the lazy eye.' I spent the next year in eye-hand coordination therapy. I had to wear a patch on one eye and perform strange exercises everyday such as crawling around the house on the floor.

Over the next two years my vision continued to deteriorate and the doctor tried numerous glasses and hard contact lenses to augment my sight, none of which worked.

Even as a young boy I possessed athletic talent. I spent every spare moment playing sports. At the end of those long summer days filled with sandlot games, I was always the last kid on the field imploring someone to stay and toss the ball as twilight trumped my glory with darkness.

I was excelling in several team sports including baseball. That vision imperfection was happening at a time when young men pride themselves in their newfound prowess of developing manhood. The sudden blunders of misjudged easy fliers and grounders were not forgiven, but often ridiculed by other players.

When my confidence should have been keeping pace with my emerging masculinity, I was quickly shattered by new inabilities.

I decided to concentrate on individual sports to avoid my embarrassment and the disappointment of letting my teammates down. I began running everyday and practicing track and field events. As I came from modest means and had little money, I tied a rope between two trees to practice high jumping.

On one particular jumping attempt, my foot became entangled in the rope and I spun through the air like a windmill and landed on my back. I noticed a man, I had never seen, mowing the neighbor's grass and observing my strange behavior. Although I did not know how long he had been watching me and could not see his expression, I was sure he must have been laughing. I was ready to give up on sports altogether.

Several days later that man, Mr. Rinehart, knocked on the door. In our driveway was a complete high jump set he had brought in the back of his truck. He had built the set himself and nothing I owned had ever looked so official. The paint stripes were perfect and regulation. Mr. Rinehart must have spent several days building that set. I was astonished and recommitted myself to track and field.

I was considered a fast runner and promising high jumper, and won several races and events early on, but the lack of vision quickly became a factor. Soon every step became a challenge. I could no longer judge the height of the bar for the high jump. I focused on running and followed the same ten-mile path everyday. When I competed at other schools, whenever possible, I would walk an unfamiliar cross-country course before a race and attempt to memorize the obstacles.

The doctor could not understand what was happening to my eyes and referred me to a specialist. At fifteen, I was diagnosed with a degenerative eye disease and the specialist informed me that I would be blind by the age of thirty.

There were over fifty students on our high school cross-country team and hundreds on the track team. Though I fell numerous times, none of the other runners knew of my challenge.

I refused to give up. That one selfless gesture by Mr. Rinehart had one big effect. Despite that I was no longer high jumping, there was this feeling that someone else had seen something in me that I had not seen myself. A complete stranger had made an investment in me and I wasn't going to let him down.

The running became my profound place of solace. I could think while I ran. I ran farther and faster everyday. The mental state I reached during these outbursts of tremendous energy became an intimate, yet ever changing place. I reached new territories of strength and motivation, but I finally could no longer see well enough to run over unfamiliar ground so I ceased competing.

By the time I reached my early twenties I had lost considerable vision in one eye and became functionally blind in the other. My one eye could read only a few pages under strain and would have to rest before I could focus again. Soon I could read only a paragraph or two, then some sentences, and within a few years I could distinguish only very large print. Many daily activities I'd taken for granted were now chores.

At twenty-six I under went surgery for my first cornea transplant. Even though the doctors made their best effort, the procedure did not succeed.

Through all of this I flatly refused to become discouraged. I worked harder to offset my shortcomings by listening more intently, taping conversations, and putting in longer hours. I copied thousands of documents, magnifying, enlarging, and then pasting them together to decipher their subject matter.

I used the English language to develop methods and acronyms to help me learn faster and remember more. My alternative measures of compensation for my poor eyesight spawned new vision.

During that time, I worked as a human resource director, consultant, salesperson, business appraiser, and business broker. I spent countless hours consulting for employers, interviewing job candidates, and investigating businesses. I saw (and heard) thousands of tax returns, financial statements, resumes, personnel files, interview notes, and policy manuals. I worked closely with many employers behind close doors where they exposed their deepest secrets. I listened.

A decade later I heard of a Doctor performing 'eyesight miracles.' I met Dr. Jay Pepose and with his skill and new technology, I had a second transplant. This time the operation was a success. Within only a few weeks, I experienced vision I had not since I was thirteen years old.

For many years trees had appeared to be green billowy forms like clouds. I had forgotten that each tree had so many individual leaves. My own face seemed that of a stranger's. Colors were at first so bright I had to wear sunglasses even indoors. The event was overwhelming.

As time passed I realized that the gradual cognizance of the rare inner perception I had gained as my eyesight had diminished, rivaled the power of the sudden impact of the revival of my eyesight.

Though I never became an Olympic high jumper or runner, Mr. Rinehart's one act and an anonymous organ donor both impressed my life and spawned chain reactions of numerous more such acts.

In a world where inhumanity sometimes seems common, never underestimate the power of any act of kindness, and allow yourself to be inspired by generous acts and modest gestures. Inspiration generates action, but must first be recognized in order to influence.

The world is rich with inspiration. Look around and you'll find there is abundance of inspiration available to everyone for free. As a job seeker, you need all the motivation and knowledge you can obtain to achieve and maintain the position and pay you want.

Become aware.
Look around you and become inspired.
Inspiration is the first step of motivation.

◆————————————◆

2. Why Employers Have Secrets

Companies spend billions of dollars for market research to understand who their customers are. Businesses want to know what features and benefits customers want in a product, how much they will pay, and how they purchase. You can only consistently sell if you comprehend why the customer buys.

The best way to understand people is get inside their minds and define their needs and desires to develop empathy. Employers are people. Employers are people making decisions. Employers are customers making decisions about what personnel to buy.

I am about to reveal to you *secret employer practices* throughout this book. Some are not very pretty. Before we condemn employers for practices that at times seem downright deceitful, we need to understand why employers behave as they do. The reason I am going to tell you these secret employer practices is so that you as a job candidate, can be better prepared by using this information to land the job you want, at the pay you deserve.

Few of the general working population realize what employers are up against. I'll explain.

Imagine this: Let's say you have a company called Company YOU. Company YOU needs a new computer.

Now in order to shop for a computer you have to place an ad in the newspaper to tell computer companies you are in the market to buy. (How you word this ad is critical as the wrong verbiage could result in a lawsuit.) After paying for an ad, within one week you receive over three hundred letters with one-page brochures in the mail from people hawking computers. Even though you stated what you wanted in your ad, every response has different specifications, software, and accessories.

The computers are used and new. New computers have not been tested and without experience no one knows if they will work. Used computers are better than new because they have track records. However, there is a high demand for these used computers so if one is available you are justified in being suspicious. Why would a good used computer be available? Was this computer 'fired' by the last owner? Does this computer just not work?

None of these letters or brochures includes any pricing. In order to buy you must call each company and arrange an appointment for a salesperson to come and explain their product. You might know what you are willing to pay but you must negotiate with each salesperson individually. The only way to purchase any computer is by paying hourly for use during the entire term of your ownership.

Depending on what industry you are in, your computer could join a union at any time and you could be forced to pay a higher hourly rate to meet the pay of a group of computers. (If you were just a consumer this might be called a monopoly, but you are considered an employer.)

When the salespeople and computers arrive for the presentation, you may only ask certain questions as allowed by law. You must stay abreast of these laws, as they are changing and new laws are enacted often. You cannot ask how old the computers are or how many times any one has been repaired. If you ask any of the wrong questions, again you could be sued.

The computer might not be compatible with any of your present equipment but there is no way to know that until after installation. The computers do not come with a warranty. No one will even guarantee delivery.

After hearing about the computers you must make a decision about which one you want and an offer of how much you can pay. The salesperson will then let you know if they accept your offer. You may be rejected because the hours you want to use the computer are not right or another customer outbid you. You may be rejected for any reason and never even know why. You would then have the choice of picking a different computer you have seen or starting the process all over again.

Here's another twist. The salespeople might not tell the truth. It's up to you to do your homework and determine whether or not they are honest. You will probably need to pay for a background check on each computer you are considering. If they have lied to you, and the computer you buy does not perform, all you can do is send the computer away and try again. If the computer has imbedded code that steals inventory from you or embezzles your money or your client's money, your only recourse is to fire the computer, send it away, possibly press charges, and start all over again.

If the computer causes damage or loss to your clients or others while in your use, you could be held liable for negligible purchasing practices.

Oh, and you will still have to pay for the time you did use the computer, even if it didn't do the job for you. You must be careful what you tell anyone about why you didn't want the computer. And when the salesperson picks up the computer, you're not allowed to erase any information that might have been placed in the computer's memory, no matter how confidential.

If at this point you're ready to cuss a blue streak, you must refrain. Your language could be construed as verbal abuse or sexual harassment.

If this sounds like a nightmare, welcome to the employer's jungle. Is it any wonder why employers have secrets? If this were the way you had to shop, wouldn't you do everything possible to protect yourself? Like:

- Requiring resumes
- Asking for references and checking them
- Requiring background checks
- Conducting more than one interview with each candidate
- Becoming an expert at the interview process

- Requiring testing
- Paying an expert consultant
- Paying a human resources department
- Conducting drug screening
- Guarding closely held secrets

Frequently, employers have gone one step further and do not actually hire the employees at all but work through a temp agency or contracted employment service. Can you blame them? In addition to the concerns presented in the analogy, employers now have a host of legal and liability issues to consider.

Now that you know *why* employers have secrets, you need to know what they are, and learn how to use them to get the job you want and pay you deserve.

◆———————————◆

During the hiring process, the job candidate can prevent the two biggest complaints employees have after only one year on the job.

3. Why You Need To Know These Secrets

So if looking for a job is like being the computer and the salesperson, and the employer has so many obstacles like Company YOU, why are the cards stacked so high against the job hunter?

Three Reasons:

1. Supply and Demand
2. Need (or desperation)
3. The Employer has Secrets

(Because the employer has so much risk)

Let's take a quick look at each of these.

1. Supply and Demand

There are almost always more job seekers than jobs. Spikes in prosperity in the economy that at the time seem like they will never end, do end. Even in these periods, there are usually more job seekers than jobs.

Current released unemployment figures are always only a small part of the picture. These figures are usually just for new jobless claims. What about the people who have run out of unemployment benefits but are still looking for work? What about the fortunate ones who never bothered to file at all (probably thinking it would be easier to get a job)? There are new graduates every year entering the job market. What about all of the people who for whatever reason are working below their previous salaries or positions and are looking to move back up? There are always people working part time who are looking for full time employment. Think about the people who are unhappy in their present positions who are looking for new jobs. Everyday new immigrants arrive to America for work. What about the companies that have decided to outsource and eliminate more positions?

Are you beginning to get the picture? As a job seeker you need every possible advantage you can get your hands on. You need to know the employer secrets to succeed at job hunting, resumes, interviews, and negotiating.

2. Need (or Desperation)

When is the worst time to look for a job? When you need one. When do most people look for a job? When they need one. Why is this the worst time to look for a job? Looking for a job when you need one puts you in the *most vulnerable or weakest position.*

When you go to a job interview needing a job, you focus on yourself. Most people have only one source of income and that is 'a job.' Therefore, when you *need* a job, all of your eggs are in one basket.

Commonly, the employer may be interviewing and selecting from hundreds of people for a single position. You are not going to make or break them. On the other hand, you may have few prospects and really need the job you are applying for. Your life could depend on getting work now.

For job hunting, interviewing, and negotiating, this puts you at the short end of the stick. From this position, I'm not sure you even have a hold of the stick. In fact, sooner or later, most likely you are going to feel like you got hit with a stick.

In most instances, if you need a job now to pay your bills next week, next month, or in the next six months, *you are desperate.* That's a strong statement! But think about this: The average amount of time a person spends looking for a job is more than three months and can be considerably longer. This is affected by economic conditions, geography, and industry. Many professional people take over a year to find the right employment. A career change can take two years or more. You could starve!

I have met very few companies that would not be able to pay their bills in the next week to three months if they did not hire a certain employee. The employer is almost always in the driver's seat and holds the cards.

Even if and when a new job is landed there are almost always no guarantees of length of employment or satisfaction. (*Imagine a job satisfaction guarantee.*) Your new job may turn out to be completely different than you expected.

Most people who need a job, blow the interview. Without specific job selling skills, *desperation always shows.*

Most people who *need* a job, end up working for less money than they are capable of earning. Without specific negotiating skills, you could be paid *considerably less*.

Most people who get a job under the condition of desperation are not satisfied with the job. Often their impression of the job is clouded by their lack of focus at the time of interviewing and hiring. They settle for less compensation than they know they are capable of earning.

Most people are *dissatisfied with their jobs within one year*. What are the two biggest complaints?

NUMBER ONE   "The job is not what I expected."

If most people are dissatisfied with their jobs within one year, and the number one complaint is the job is different than the employee expected, then the majority of job candidates are not accurately assessing the employer or the position.

NUMBER TWO "I am not making enough money."

If anyone is not making enough money after only one year on the job, unless the employer has reneged on a raise or initiated a substantial pay cut, which is not likely, the employee has no one to blame but him or her self. Either the job candidate accepted a job with inadequate pay, or did not negotiate effectively.

What can you do to avoid these situations? You can read and learn the employer secrets and use the 'job selling' skills and negotiating tactics described in this book. You need to know what employer secrets are and how to use them to *make sure you are offered the job you want, want the job you're offered, and get the money you deserve.*

QUICK- Remember the title to this book?

Employer Secrets

And

How to Use Them To Get

The Job and Pay YOU Want

The secrets in this book and the methods of how to use them are to help YOU get the JOB and PAY you want. By knowing how to ask the right questions, you can determine if the job is right for you or not.

Now that you know why employers have secrets you might imagine at what lengths they will go to develop and protect their advertising, resume screening, interviewing, hiring, and negotiating secrets.

3. Employer Secrets

Employers might spend one thousand times more money to hire you than you spend to get a job. Most employer secrets are designed to protect them and increase their odds of success.

Your awareness of employer practices and possessing the knowledge to deal with them will increase your odds of success.

After years of consulting and delving into the deepest business secrets of employer practices, I know that if you're not aware of these practices and have the skills to deal with them, the cards are stacked against you.

The secrets and methods exposed in this book will help you turn that stack of cards in to a *house of cards*, and if you have ever built one, you know how easily a house of cards will fall!

◆━━━━━━━━━━◆

4. The Lesson That Cost Me $100,000. (That Could Make You a Million)

Early in my career I had been out of work for several months and was low on funds. I admit that's an understatement. I was driving around on a donut tire because I couldn't afford to fix a flat! A local company was advertising for a professional position that I was perfectly qualified for. I had sent a resume and got the call for an interview.

Upon arriving at the interview I was filled with an exciting anxiety, like a coin flipping in my stomach with a paycheck on one side and a stern interviewer asking tough questions on the other. I sat in front of a well-dressed lady asking me questions that I answered quickly as I anticipated the moment of truth - *How much was I going to make?*

Ms. Trump then took me on a tour of the business, with introductions to several department managers. Within ten minutes I could not have told you one persons' name that I had been introduced to, including hers, or what the new product was they were all buzzing about. But to this day I can tell you the exact annual salary, the bonus percentage, the number of holidays, and weeks of vacation allowance. The job paid more than I had ever made.

Because of my qualifications I was called back for a second interview. This time Ms. Trump brought a senior executive into the room. He introduced himself and asked me one question:

"Who do you feel is the best target market for our new product?"

This resulted in me stammering, and then him questioning her as to why she hadn't told me about their new product, and her defending herself by stating that she did tell me about it. A second interview for a promising dream position was now turning into one of my most embarrassing moments.

After the senior executive left, Ms. Trump asked me why I hadn't answered him. I told her the truth. I had not been paying attention. She told me she had expected to offer me the position that day. She was impressed with my experience. Her last words to me were, "I was almost sold." I apologized and said goodbye.

I really blew it. I was not getting the job because of my own desperation. Like many people, I had been desperate and lacking interview knowledge and 'job selling' skills. I was focused on my own needs and myself. In fact so much so, that I didn't pay attention to what the employer was saying about what she needed.

As I often do and as painful as the process can be, I went home and wrote down the whole experience hoping to learn something. That night I tossed and turned as her last words kept me awake, "I was almost sold."

Obviously I made the mistake of not listening and had forgotten that I was there for another purpose besides my own. But as I repeated her last words to myself I realized the single, *most powerful*, job-hunting lesson I have ever known.

The Greatest Job Hunting Principle
When you are looking for a job:
You are the service or product.
The employer is the customer.
You are selling.
The employer is buying.

It's that simple! You are the product. The employer is your customer. The employer is going to pay for you. The cover letter and resume are your advertising. How you get your resume out is your marketing.

The interview is your product presentation. This is your chance to perform. The general format of an interview, which is when the employer asks the questions and the candidate provides the answers, is completely backwards. Selling is about learning your customer's needs and desires and persuading them that you can fulfill those needs and desires. How can you learn anything about someone who is asking all the questions? By using the 'job selling' skills in this book.

You are the product. You know your product better than anyone. Only you can analyze your customer's needs and decide whether or not you can meet them.

Employer Secret 61: Employers hire the wrong people, keep the wrong people, promote the wrong people, and fire the wrong people, *everyday*. (Employers work very hard to keep this a secret.)

What's important to you is that putting the interests of your prospective employer (customer) first is in your best interest. The hiring decision is as much your responsibility as the employer. By using the ideas and methods I have outlined in this book, you will be in a much better position to decide if the job is right for you and you are right for the job. One more time! When you are looking for a job:

> *You are the service or product.*
> *The employer is the customer.*
> *You are selling.*
> *The employer is buying.*

The more I incorporated this philosophy into all aspects of job hunting and consulting, the more offers came pouring in. As of today, I have personally turned down more jobs than I have accepted by many times over.

As an employer, I have watched as numerous candidates have made the same mistake I did of thinking about themselves and not focusing on the employer. By showing job hunters the short cuts of 'job selling' described later in this book, I have helped countless people get the job they wanted at the pay they deserved.

Focusing on the employer is the most important and powerful 'job-hunting attitude.'

In the Company YOU story, people came to you to conduct a sales presentation of their computer. You were the customer.

When you apply for a job, the employer is the customer. In my interview, I had so grossly ignored this fact I did not even listen to what my 'customer' was saying.

If this concept is so simple then why does the interview process seem backwards?

Because most employers…
- dictate the interview.
- *think* they know what's best for themselves.
- are not always the best listeners.
- think the interview is only about them and what they want.
- don't always know what their company needs.
- DO NOT REALLY CARE what the employee wants or needs (Sad but true, what employees want or need is not at the top of the priority list of most employers' concerns.)

<u>And because most job seekers…</u>
- believe the interview is about them and what they want.
- don't know what the employer wants.
- DO NOT REALLY CARE what the employer wants or needs (Sad but true).
- are not expert salespeople or even good at selling.
- do not know how to truly focus on an employer's needs and desires.
- lack the knowledge and therefore the confidence to take control of the interview and are intimidated by the hiring process. This is because most people don't understand what hiring is really about.

I repeat, selling is about learning your customer's needs and desires and persuading them that you can fulfill those needs and desires. Getting a job is about selling. *You must have 'job selling' skills.* Even though 'job selling' skills include most basic selling skills, additional and specific 'job selling' skills are required because of the structure of the interview.

How could all this *make you a million?* My mistake probably cost me much more than $ 100,000. If I would have kept that job for say ten years, with any raises or bonuses the sum could have been well over one million dollars. When you look for a job think about the BIG picture. Ask yourself how long you estimate you will stay with that employer. Multiply the annual job pay and benefits times the number of years. At minimum, that's an estimate of what the job is to worth to you.

The important question for job hunting is: How much are you worth to the customer (employer)?

The more you focus on the employer as a customer the less you focus on yourself. The less you focus on yourself the less apt you are to be nervous and the more confident you become. The more confident you are the more capable you become.

The better your 'job selling' skills are the better employee you will be. The better your 'job selling' skills are the more money you will make. The better your 'job selling' skills are, the better the odds that you will be able to pick the right employer and be happy with your job.

◆——————————◆

Section I Summary

Three Reasons The Cards are Stacked Against the Job
Hunter
1. Supply and Demand
2. Need (or desperation)
3. The Employer has Secrets
(Because the employer has so much risk)

Because of supply and demand, desperation, and
employer secrets, *you must have ' job selling' skills.*

Putting the best interests of your prospective employer
first is in your best interest.

Most people are *dissatisfied with their jobs within one
year.*
What are the two biggest complaints?

1. "The job is not what I expected."

*If most people are dissatisfied with their jobs within one
year, and the number one complaint is the job is different
than the employee expected, then the majority of job
candidates are not accurately assessing the employer or
the position.*

2. "I am not making enough money."

If anyone is not making enough money after only one year on the job, unless the employer has initiated a substantiul pay cut, which is not likely, the employee has no one to blame but him or her self. Either they accepted a job with inadequate pay, or they did not negotiate effectively.

When you are looking for a job:

You are the service or product.

The employer is the customer.

You are selling.

The employer is buying.

It's that simple!

▼▼▼▼▼▼▼▼▼▼▼▼▼▼▼▼▼▼▼▼▼▼▼▼▼▼▼▼▼▼▼▼

Listening is what talking is all about.

II. Employer Secrets and Job Selling Skills

People buy when they perceive the value of what they are buying to be worth at least what they are parting with.

5. My Four Simple Steps To 'Job Selling'

A business client telephoned me and asked if his daughter's best friend, Jennifer, could schedule an appointment with me. She had recently graduated from college and was having trouble finding a job. I asked him how long she had been looking for work and he said "for almost two months." He must have detected the sarcasm in my voice when I responded with "two whole months?"

My friend told me Jennifer was an accounting major and explained that the interviewing was the challenge for her. She would get very nervous, her palms would sweat, and she would have trouble concentrating.

I scheduled the appointment. When Jennifer arrived at my office, I was on the telephone and noticed she was fidgety while waiting. I finished my call and introduced myself.

"Didn't you just graduate from college in May?" I asked.

"Yes," she responded sheepishly.

"… And you majored in business?"

"Yes."

"Weren't you required to take any public speaking classes?"

"Yes," she stated, "and I did very well."

"Then why do you think you are so nervous during job interviews?"

"I'm not sure," she replied. "I have been to seven job interviews that have all gone the same way"

"How's that?" I inquired.

Jennifer explained the interview scenario. She would answer a barrage of similar questions and be told to expect a call that never came.

I had her answer a few typical interview questions and listened to her rehearsed, robot like answers.

I told her the 'Company YOU' story and I could see by the way her head lifted and she made eye contact that I had her attention. She was intrigued.

"Why I never thought of it that way. These poor employers." She responded. "All of this time I have concentrated all of my thoughts on myself."

"These poor employers don't need sympathy Jennifer, they need empathy. Job interviews are about selling. Prospective companies are your customers."

"I racked up the bills during school. I had been 'waitressing' part time but the restaurant closed. I really *need* a job. How do I go from thinking so much about myself to focusing on the employer's needs?" she asked.

"You leap," I answered.

"I do what?'

"You leap."

I then handed her a 3x5 card I keep on my desk. I had written these words several years before:

THE FOUR SIMPLE STEPS OF SELLING
To Get From Self Focus to Customer Focus Just...

LEAP

Learn
Empathize
Assess
Persuade

Learn your customer's needs and desires.
Empathize with their position.
Assess if you *can and want* to meet their needs and desires.
Persuade your customer that you can *help them* meet those needs and desires better than anyone else on the planet.

"Jennifer, put yourself in the employer's shoes. In our analogy of Company YOU, if you were convinced that I could supply the computer and service you wanted, better than anyone on the planet, would you buy from me?" I asked.

"Of course," she replied, " and it seems to me if you could do that you would win every time."

"Almost," I responded.

"I'm not sure I can convince employers that I can meet their needs and desires better than anyone else on the planet," she stated.

"I'm not sure you can't. Even so, I don't think you always have to. That is the goal, however people buy when they perceive the value of what they are buying to be worth what they are parting with," I informed her.

"In other words, they'll hire me when they believe I can do the job for what they are willing to pay?" Jennifer asked.

"Yes."

Jennifer read the card again, aloud. "I have gone to these interviews knowing very little about the companies," she said.

"Learning has a mighty side effect," I stated.

"What side effect?"

"Confidence," I explained.

"That's what I need!" she exclaimed.

"What size companies have you been applying to?" I asked.

"They have all been larger companies. Does that matter?"

"Did you know that right now, small businesses generate the most new jobs?"

"Aren't small businesses more risky? Can small businesses afford to pay what the big companies can? How do I know how big or small a business is?"

"Slow down Jennifer!" I could see she was becoming more enthusiastic and less nervous.

"Small businesses can be splendid opportunities. They are often much more flexible, and can sometimes pay more based on performance. Commonly, small business owners today have only one tier or no middle management. Do not rule out large companies; just start seeking out the smaller ones. There are numerous ways to determine the size of businesses."

At this time, small businesses generate the most new jobs in the US.

Employer Secret 59: Small businesses usually appreciate wider skill sets.

Employer Secret 60: People in larger businesses often fear wider skill sets.

Jennifer's enthusiasm led her to become a student of LEAP. She learned that focusing on the employer (and others) generated self-confidence. She used the principles of LEAP as outlined in the next several chapters to get the job she wanted and advance to an upper management position within two years.

Review

THE FOUR SIMPLE STEPS OF SELLING

Learn your customer's needs and desires.
Empathize with their position.
Assess if you can *and want* to meet their needs and desires.
Persuade them that you can meet those needs and desires better than anyone else on the planet.

6. How To Spy on Them

The first step of LEAP.
Learn your customer's needs and desires.

First learn *who* your customer is.

Larry, a minister friend of mine, was scheduled to interview for a new position at a church with a fairly large congregation. This would be only his second job and he came to me for advice.

During our discussion I could sense that he was nervous about the interview. He told me that he was to spend a half an hour with the present minister and then meet with the church board of twenty members.

I have mixed feelings about interviews with predecessors. Present employees are sometimes resentful about being replaced and if you appear too good, they may not like the idea of you taking their role.

"Larry, one way I have found to minimize anxiety and increase confidence is through knowledge. Learn more about these people and who they are," I informed him.

"How can I do that?" he questioned.

"Spy on them."

"Spy on a church?" he retorted, "How?"

"When is your interview?"

"In two weeks."

"Attend their services this Sunday and sit at the back of the church."

Larry did just that. Later he told me that he found the minister to be down to earth and uplifting. He said the congregation was warm and friendly.

"After my visit, I couldn't wait for the interview," he said.

It's not always this easy to see inside of a business. There are plenty of ways to get inside information though.

Start with learning everything you can about the prospective customer (prospective employer). In order to learn what your customer needs and wants, you need knowledge. There are several ways to obtain the information needed to assess the customer's situation.

What to Know Before the Interview

First, learn all you can before the interview. Before you walk in to any job interview you should know the answers to most of the following questions:

- What exactly does the company do?
- How many employees do they have?
- What is their annual gross revenue?
- Is the company closely held or publicly traded?
- Is it a government entity?
- Who is the president or owner of the company?
- Who are their major competitors?

- Who is their typical customer?
- Are you being interviewed by the owner, a department head, manager, human resource employee, or hiring agency?

The richest source of information about any company is at the company. When practical, you should drive to the employer a day or two before the interview. Park outside where you can see employees leaving at the end of the day. See what kind of moods they are in and how they dress.

- Make a call to the Better Business Bureau and check the employer's reputation.
- Research the business online.
- Go to the library and search for past local newspaper articles about the company.
- Get a copy of their annual report.
- Get their product brochures.
- Visit their distributors.
- Visit their competition.
- Eat lunch where they eat lunch.

The Walls Can Talk

The interview is a great opportunity for you to become an observation sponge. When going to an interview arrive early and carouse the building. Observe the parking, the cars, the building, and the signs. Inside notice the décor, the workspaces, the lighting, the periodicals in the lobby, and whatever you see.

If you spend time waiting within earshot of a receptionist or other employees, listen to what's happening.

Employer Secret 48: Employers hide the work environment.

One way employers hide the work environment is by conducting off-site interviews. Never accept any job offer without seeing the environment you will be working in.

I have been so bold to ask for a copy of the company policies and procedures manual. Although you might not get one before, at, or after an interview, you should always get a copy after an offer is made and before you have accepted the job.

For more information on investigating companies visit:
www.employersecrets.com

◆———————————◆

7. Never Go to an Interview To Get a Job

More on the first step of LEAP.
Learn your customer's needs and desires.

Job interviews are sales presentations and s*ales presentations are about the customer, not just you or your product.* Yes the customer (interviewer) wants to know more about the product, you, but only from the perspective of their needs and desires. The only way you can analyze your customer's needs and desires is if you know exactly what they are. The qualified job candidate who leaves the interview knowing the most about the company, people, and opening will have the advantage and be in the top running for the job. Be prepared to provide information but go to an interview to learn.

Going to an interview to get a job says:

I am here because *I want something from you.*

Going to an interview to learn says:

I am here because *I want to give you something.*

As simple as this concept is, implementation takes hard work. I have practiced selling for a long time and have learned to become absorbed with the interests of my customers. My personal and financial rewards are far more abundant now than when my own interests were at the forefront of my thoughts and actions.

There are numerous roadblocks to the regular practice of putting other's interests first. Three that top the list are selfishness, laziness, and shortsightedness.

Selfishness is one of the most self-defeating human states. Some people will never figure out they are not the earth's axis.

Many people are too shortsighted to see the end reward they will receive for putting other people first. They want instant gratification.

Some people have put other's interests first and been burned. In most instances these people were not aware of the boundaries required. Putting other people's interests first does not mean you abandon your own interests.

A job interview is your opportunity to learn about your customer's needs and determine if you can and want to fulfill them. Let's learn from the sales pros. The biggest mistake sales people make is talking too much. The biggest interview mistake job candidates make is talking too much. *Almost every answer should be limited to three sentences or less.*

The Nine Lessons of Listening Science

A winning job candidate needs to be familiar with 'Listening Science.'

The first three 'Lessons of Listening Science' are:

> **Lesson One**   *Shut up*
> **Lesson Two**   *Shut up*
> **Lesson Three** *Shut up*

Once while training salespeople, I listened while they worked with prospects in the showroom. One particular salesperson, Kevin, was a top producer. Yet I found that he was still missing numerous opportunities by not listening and not remembering when he did listen. His energy level was usually several steps above his customer's. More than once I heard customers say "Okay, we'll buy one," and he would keep right on talking and they would excuse themselves and leave in a hurry.

Many of these same customers would sneak back into the store later and buy from a different salesperson. This resulted in several challenging situations, as these were commission only salespeople.

During an interview I have made the decision to hire candidates and before I could tell them, their non-stop chatter talked me out of making the offer.

Listening Science Lesson Four
Ask Questions.

A salesperson must know the when, what, why, and how to ask questions. Asking questions serves several purposes:

- Asking questions gets the other person talking and you listening.
- Asking questions puts you in control.
- Asking questions gets you information
- Asking questions helps you develop empathy.
- Asking questions develops trust.

Questions are the POWER of conversation. Most people like to talk and most people like to talk about themselves. Getting the other person to talk gets you information, helps you gain control of the conversation, and increases the time you will be listening and not talking.

I have discovered one very interesting side effect of listening: The more someone *talks to you* the more they *trust you.*

<u>Key Questions You Should be Asking</u>
1. Have you had the opportunity to review my resume?
2. What did you see in my resume that made you call me?
3. Is this a new position?
4. What skills would the perfect candidate have?
5. What are the ways you measure the productivity of this position?
6. How soon do you plan on hiring someone?
7. What are the critical issues that require immediate attention?
8. How many people do you expect to interview for this position?
9. How long have you been with the company?
10. Is there someone in addition to you that will make the hiring decision?
11. Who would be doing my job in the event of my vacation absence?

12. Would I be expected to perform anyone else's duties in the event of another employee's absence?
13. Do you have a policy and procedures manual? (Could I see it?)
14. Who would I be reporting to?
15. What are the parameters of authority for this position?

Listening Science Lesson Five

Ask pertinent questions.

The question samples herein are only samples. Although you can have prepared and rehearsed questions, NEVER script questions to be asked in a specific or exact order. When someone answers your question, the answer should spawn your next question. Your next question should be relative to their answer.

Employer Secret 71: Some employers use two-way mirrors to observe interviews.

During a consulting job with a two-way mirror, I witnessed the following interview. See if you can figure out what's wrong with this picture.

Interviewer: "Did you ever work on job sites without supervision while supervising others?"

Candidate: "Yes I do sometimes. My boss often leaves the job site. He knows that I am looking for another position. How soon do you need someone?"

Interviewer: "We would like to start as soon as we find the right person. Could you tell me about some of those jobs?"

Candidate: Which jobs?

Interviewer: " Where you supervised others."

Candidate: "Oh Yes. We are now completing a new elementary school. The project has gone very well. I have six of the latest certifications and an electrician's license as well. Is that important to you?"

Interviewer: "Yes. We need someone that can make decisions for others and work on site without supervision. Could you tell me about a time when you had to make a difficult decision alone about an employee?"

Candidate: "Most of my employees work long hours and have not been too difficult. I plan their schedules. I can work long hours too. I am also available weekends. Do you have a lot of overtime work?"

Interviewer: "Sometimes."

Candidate: "I am dependable and do not miss work. What current issues do you have that need to be solved?"

Interviewer: "We really would like a person who is qualified enough to make decisions independently. We have a crew of five that needs job site supervision. How would any one of the employees you are supervising now describe you?

Candidate: "They're a good group. How long have you been here with this company?"

Is this candidate at the same interview as the interviewer? The interviewer is looking for assurance that this candidate can work as an independent supervisor. After several attempts the interviewer gave up.

Questions should flow like conversation. In order for this to happen, when you ask a question you must be listening attentively to the answers.

Employer Secret 43: Interviewers do not want to pull teeth. If they are not getting the answers they are looking for from you, or if the conversation goes off track early, they will eliminate you.

Listening Science Lesson Six
Relate to Them.

Relating to people, or finding common ground helps them better identify with you and helps you empathize with them. Learning that the interviewer and you both belong to the same organization, have similar interests or hobbies can make conversation flow easier.

There is a fine line between finding common ground and trying to become instant friends. Do not try to 'chum up' with an interviewer. Noticing from her degree on the wall that you both went to the same college warrants mention to establish common ground, but not to pursue old college stories. Interviewers want and need to remain professional and do not like surprises.

Common ground is great as long as you don't trespass the property line. You do not want to get involved in personal discussions and discover during your college days you dated the interviewer's spouse, for example.

Most interviewers are cautious of hiring anyone with which they might have a connection that could later be interpreted as a conflict of hiring interest.

Listening Science Lesson Seven
Be interested in what they are saying.

Focusing on what another person is saying and timely responding with pertinent questions demonstrates interest.

Listening Science Lesson Eight
Remember What They've Said.

During my period of very poor vision, I would listen to people intently (I hope I still do). I would take numerous mental notes. I cannot later recall even a ten-minute conversation verbatim. I practice remembering the key points that tell me about the other party's needs and desires.

Employer Secret 7: Numerous employers tape interviews.

You can too. A small digital tape recorder can be kept in a purse or shirt pocket.

I find listening to myself later to be difficult. I don't sound like I think and I am critical of every sentence I have uttered. But listening to my interviews has dramatically improved my interview skills.

Listening to your recorded interview will also help you later in the negotiation process.

Listening Science Lesson Nine

Timing is critical. You must know when to ask questions.

Your questions must be relevant to the subject of conversation at the moment. Questions must flow as if a natural part of the conversation. Timing is critical.

Do not walk in to an interview firing a barrage of questions. As a job candidate, I always respond to the first three to five questions before I ask a question. I limit my answers to 'yes' or 'no' or less than three sentences. Then I answer each question and ask a *pertinent* question at the end of my answer.

Don't wait for the interviewer to invite you to ask questions. I have observed plenty of interviews where the interviewer does *not* give the candidate an opportunity to ask questions.

◆————————◆

Walking a mile in other people's shoes
will probably only make you think their feet hurt.

8. The BIGGEST Selling and Life Lesson I Know

The Second Step of LEAP
Empathize With Their Position

I have never taken a class in empathy nor am I aware of one. The definition seems easy enough:

> To identify with and understand
> another's feelings, situation, or motive.

Maybe most people assume that since this seems to be such an easy concept, everyone must understand and experience empathy. Or maybe most people assume that empathy is an instinct or trait everyone is born with. This is not the case. Our prisons are overcrowded with violent criminals, many who confess they have no remorse for their victims. I'm not stating that an understanding of empathy and the ability to fully experience true empathy would eliminate violent crime. I do believe if everyone would at least have some lessons in practicing empathy, we would see a reduction in people's harm against their fellow person and greater personal success.

One misconception is that empathy produces only compassion, an understanding of suffering. Empathy is often interpreted only as sympathy. In some dictionaries, *pity* is even listed as a synonym of empathy.

The process of empathy involves defining, understanding, and producing emotions.

Even people who perceive empathy often make no effort to practice this feeling. Capitalism engenders a creed of self-gratification where empathy seems to serve little purpose. Advertising, the sustenance of free enterprise, has become pervasive yet absent of messages of true empathy.

The same feverish competition of capitalism is supreme in society's pastimes. Contests, game shows, and a myriad of sports, display little or no signs of empathy. Because empathy is so misunderstood most sports players and fans would find such a demonstration weak and offensive. At best, a display of good sportsmanship is acceptable. Therefore, there is no surprise that any emotion or emotion producing process such as empathy, so seemingly disregarded by society, would not be common in the day-to-day interactions of business.

How ironic that advertisers work so hard to spark emotion and that people become so emotional about sports and competitions, that a process designed to communicate, transfer, and experience the emotions of others would be so shunned.

I enjoy competition as much as any participant or spectator ever has; yet I have found true effective empathy my greatest tool in business and contention.

I did not succeed with empathy immediately. After seeing modest success practicing only the basic definition of empathy, in my relentless pursuit of reaching my vocational and personal potential, I became a student of empathy.

I discovered that my empathy was in vain if the party had no need or desire for what I had to offer.

Initially, I attempted to exercise empathy from my own best interests. Soon I discovered that this was an oxymoron of egocentric empathy. This mistake caused me to misinterpret the needs and desires of others and cost me plenty.

In other instances, although I thought I was practicing empathy, I was making many assumptions from my own perspective that were impeding complete success.

Sometimes I met people in situations I had not been in. I did not relate to what they were feeling. I would imagine how I would react or feel in their situation. Although this is a good start and a commonly perceived complete definition of practicing empathy, with sayings such as 'put your self in their shoes,' I found that my feet often did not 'fit' in their shoes.

I realized empathy was much more difficult to practice with consistent victory than I had first believed, yet I persisted.

I discovered that before I simply placed myself in someone's shoes and imagined how I would feel and react, I *first needed to understand and respond to how they were feeling or reacting.*

After years of study and practice, I developed these three principles to use as steps to 'effective empathy' as shown in order:

'The Three Principle Steps to Effective Empathy'

STEP ONE

First, you must determine *if* the other person has a need or desire. A *qualified* need or desire that *you can and want* to fulfill.

STEP TWO

Secondly, you must see the other person's need or desire *from his or her perspective or best interests*. This is informed empathy. This is critical.

STEP THREE

Third, you need to relate their need or desire with the closest need or desire of your own in order to *invoke the same or at least similar feelings within yourself.*

I shall explain:

Let's say you are far out at sea standing on the deck of a cruise ship full of passengers. You are hundreds of miles from shore and there is no other watercraft in sight.

You see a man adrift in the water a few dozen feet from the ship. You rush to the side and throw him a life preserver that lands within his reach. You are sure that the preserver is the only chance he has to survive. He looks at you and refuses to grab hold.

How would you persuade him? You might say, "Grab the preserver or you will drown!" A person in a healthy state of mind who was drowning would certainly oblige your request. His desire would be motivated by the fear of loss of life. However maybe he had jumped off of your ship intentionally.

If he still did not take hold of the preserver what would you do? Maybe keep yelling. You do and he still doesn't move. Maybe he is standing atop a submarine hidden just below the surface.

Next you begin yelling in other languages. You try speaking Spanish and French, and then you begin recruiting passengers that might speak more languages.

You are certainly making a gallant effort. But in each instance you are thinking in terms of his interests from your perspective. So in order to persuade someone to do something, we must first determine their need or desire *from their perspective.*

In each case all the yelling and convincing in the world might not work in the wrong language or if the man in the water was deaf. Persuasion will often not work if the need or desire has not been properly identified or is from the wrong perspective. Persuasion will not work if there is no need for what you are offering.

By practicing the first step of LEAP, learning your customer's needs and desires, you gather the information to develop empathy.

If you asked the man in the water why he was there, he might have answered you and saved you some time and frustration. If he answered you by saying he was drowning, but had no arms with which to grasp the life preserver, you could react differently.

When you threw the man the life preserver you were acting with empathy. Just not informed empathy. (However in such an emergency situation I would have responded just as you did. By the way, congratulations, you performed an action without any expectation of reward!)

The reason you would throw a life preserver to a person whom you presumed was drowning is easy. You identify as a human on the elementary level of fear, which in this case is loss of life.

The need or desire of your customer (prospective employer) might not be so easy to understand or identify with. You might not have ever taken the risk of hiring someone before. How can you empathize with a need or desire you have never had?

UNDERSTANDING PRINCIPLE THREE

You need to relate your prospective employer's need or desire with the closest need or desire of your own in order to *invoke the same or similar feelings within yourself.*

This final stage to the process of reaching effective empathy has helped me truly relate to people in a way I once thought was impossible. The purpose of the analogy of the Company YOU story in Chapter Two is to invoke empathy in the reader or job seeker, you, for what employers are facing in the hiring process.

Empathy is not sympathy.
Sympathy can be a product of empathy.
Empathy is about understanding.

The first 'empathy relation statements' in Chapter Two about Company YOU were:

- Employers are people.
- Employers are people making decisions.
- Employers are customers making decisions about what staff to buy.

This much is easy. We are all people. We have all made decisions. We have all been customers. As the analogy progressed, as a customer who has made decisions, you probably understood the frustration employers feel in the hiring process.

To develop genuine and effective empathy, identify your customer's need or desire and think of the closest need or desire you have or have experienced in order to *invoke the same or similar feelings within yourself.*

Identifying a customer's needs and desires is not always hard, yet I have found some cases to be formidable mysteries.

One sunny Friday afternoon, I was driving on a stretch of back road, two-lane highway with little traffic, on my way to prepare for a closing on a steel fabrication plant. I was the broker for the sale. The seller was retiring and the buyers were a younger couple with experience working for a similar company. The buyers had completed their due diligence and were excited about their new venture.

After several months of work in which negotiations had gone well and all financing had been obtained, we would be closing the following Monday morning. I would receive a hefty commission check Monday that would pay all of my bills for the next year. I just needed to inspect some assets for serial numbers and pick up a final inventory list from the seller.

Everything was so right with my world I was whistling as I stopped at a small produce stand and picked up a watermelon for a picnic on the weekend.

When I arrived at the plant, for the first time the seller, Mr. Jenkins, did not greet me with the usual smile. As I collected serial numbers he followed me around the plant. When we arrived at an older delivery pick up truck he stated, 'This truck doesn't go with the business. It belongs to me personally."

"Mr. Jenkins," I started slowly, "isn't this truck on the asset list we have already given to the buyers?" (I knew that it was.)

"I don't think so," he responded. "...and it doesn't matter if it is."

Mr. Jenkins made the same claim about a drill press, a computer, and several desks. He then handed me a list of work in progress and he wanted the buyers to reimburse him for material purchases. Upon further inquiry I learned that all of the work in progress had been started from material that had already been included in the inventory list. If the buyers met this request they would be paying him twice for the same material.

Mr. Jenkins told me he had taken an order the day before that had to get out and a cutting shear needed to be repaired to produce the goods. The cost was five thousand seven hundred dollars and since the buyers were buying the assets in 'as is' condition, and they had inspected everything earlier in the week, he felt they should have to pay for the repair. I reminded Mr. Jenkins that he had told the buyers all machinery and equipment was in good working order.

As I drove home my head was in a spin. I knew the buyers were going to be furious. Mr. Jenkins's unfair and unreasonable behavior could blow the whole transaction.

When I returned to the office I called the buyers. They certainly were furious. "How could anyone be such a selfish greedy jerk?" 'Jerk" was some of the better language I heard. They would not pay the same price for the business with fewer assets than promised and unless I could do something the deal was off. I assured them I would have everything straightened out by eleven o'clock Monday morning for the closing.

I did not sleep well that night nor did I enjoy my picnic that weekend. I kept thinking about all the work I had put into this deal and how much I wanted the commission.

"How could anyone be such a selfish greedy jerk?" I thought. Later at home I got a pencil and note pad, as I often do when I am in turmoil, and found a quiet place to relax. I stared at the blank paper for a long time and then I wrote in large block letters across the top of the page:

HOW COULD ANYONE BE SUCH A SELFISH GREEDY JERK?

I remembered when I first met Mr. Jenkins; he certainly hadn't seemed like a selfish greedy jerk. In all of our meetings and negotiations he had never once behaved like a selfish greedy jerk. He had told me about a charity organization he supports, he had volunteered an extra month of free training to the buyers, and bought my lunch twice.

As I stared at my writing I realized that what I had written on the paper was not a statement but a question.
I wrote the question again like this:

IIOW COULD **MR. JENKINS** BE SUCH A SELFISH GREEDY JERK?

And again like this....
HOW COULD MR. JENKINS **ACT LIKE** SUCH A SELFISH GREEDY JERK?

I made a list of what I knew about Mr. Jenkins.
- *He is 72 years old.*
- *He started with nothing and has worked hard all of his life with no vacations.*
- *He is married and his wife wants him to retire. She wants to travel.*
- *His children are all grown and not interested in taking over his business.*

I then imagined how he must feel at his age in his position and what he might be thinking.

I wrote down the following conclusions.
- *He is probably concerned about his future.*
- *He is leaving his daily routine for an unfamiliar life style.*
- *He probably has not learned how to relax.*
- *He might feel he will no longer be productive.*

- *His retirement is a big step toward his impending mortality.*
- *He, like most people, does not want to change.*
- *He does not want to let go.*
- *He might try to hang on to material objects for reassurance.*
- *He might think this was his last chance to make any money ever again.*
- *He is afraid.*
- *He does not want to admit that he is afraid.*

Even though these might seem like simple and logical conclusions, in order to reach them I had to stop thinking about myself and start thinking about Mr. Jenkins. Only by allowing myself to see his needs and desires from his perspective, at age seventy-two, did I begin to understand.

Then I related to Mr. Jenkins' feelings of fear with my own. I thought about my fear of losing this deal and how I would feel if this were the last deal I would ever be making. My original anxiety over my commission check seemed much smaller now in comparison to what Mr. Jenkins must be feeling. I now had a feeling of empathy for Mr. Jenkins. How could I take action that would help assure Mr. Jenkins?

Mr. Jenkins had made some unfair demands on Friday, but I knew that he was not a selfish greedy jerk. I had to get Mr. Jenkins to see how unfair he was behaving without having to expose his feelings. The best way I could think of to get Mr. Jenkins to come to reason was the same way I had understood him. He would need some empathy for the buyers.

Instead of feeling distraught about the possibility of losing a sizable commission I was now charged with energy. Sunday night I reached Mrs. Jenkins at their home.

"Mrs. Jenkins this is Phil Baker. It would be a personal favor to me if you could bring any pictures of you and your family and your husband's business from the early days to my office in the morning before the closing. Anything at all that you have would be fine. I will copy the pictures and return them to you."

The next morning Mr. and Mrs. Jenkins arrived with an envelope that had over three dozen pictures of the family and business from the early building stages of the plant and spanning over several years.

I told the Jenkins I wanted to give the buyers a picture album to capture memories of their business and what better way to start than with some of the company's beginnings.

As I looked through the pictures I asked questions about each one and watched as a proud glow appeared on Mr. Jenkins' face when he responded. He spoke of the struggles they had encountered and referred to those trying periods as the best times of their lives.

I pointed out how our buyers were sure to be having many of the same feelings and how they had hocked everything to buy this business and would appreciate any help. Mrs. Jenkins smiled and held her husband's hand. "Why with his help these new owners will surely succeed."

On the way to the closing I mentioned to Mr. Jenkins that the items he had wanted to keep were already on the asset list. His response was, "Oh I thought they might be. Well they'll need those things to get going. I don't know what I would have done with them anyway."

I deposited my check that afternoon.

By stopping, writing my thoughts, and contemplating the situation, I had learned some lessons that became far more valuable than that commission.

- By practicing empathy you can identify the true motivating emotions behind the behavioral mask.
- You can induce empathy in another person through references they identify with, to inspire persuasion.
- Practicing effective true empathy can help put your emotions into perspective and have a positive affect on your state of mind.
- In order to understand the thinking of your buyer you must know yourself.

I also learned to face some tough things about myself. You can only empathize with a buyer's emotion or desire if you understand it yourself. The easiest way to understand another person's emotion or desire is to have had one the same or similar. As all motivations are not necessarily good, practicing empathy can force us to face some uncomfortable feelings about ourselves. Admitting and experiencing my fear of losing my commission, although undesirable, allowed me to begin to comprehend the fear of my seller.

People often label behavior without looking for the motivational feeling or cause. Bad behavior is labeled as greedy, selfishness, jealousy, vengeful, or just by names such as 'jerk.' To produce empathy we have to identify the true motivating feeling behind the behavioral mask.

Mr. Jenkins was acting like a jerk, selfish and uncaring. I have observed the following behavioral masks and discovered the most probable motivational feelings as shown.

Behavioral Mask	Motivating Feelings
Greed -----------------------	Insecurity/Fear
Selfishness -----------------	Insecurity/Fear
Jealousy ---------------------	Pain/Fear of Loss
Vengeful --------------------	Anger/Pain
Anger -----------------------	Pain/Fear
Inflated Ego ----------------	Insecurity/Fear

Identifying the motivational feelings behind the behavior does not condone or condemn conduct. This only supports the process of 'effective empathy.'

At first consideration, an interview might not seem to allow for analysis of this depth. After practice, I have found 'effective empathy' can be practiced in almost any situation and become invaluable throughout the hiring process, pay negotiations, and employment.

Thinking in other people's best interests does not mean you abandon your own interests or sacrifice them. Thinking in other people's best interests *enhances your chances* of satisfying your interests.

Many salespeople have been trained to use the first principle of 'Effective Empathy' and determine a customer's need or desire. They look for the buyer's 'hot buttons.' This is not hard and can be done in conversation usually by asking a few questions.

Still often, as soon as salespeople find these hot buttons they stop and began describing the benefits of their product that seem to satisfy the customer's need. This is where I have seen a considerable number of sales fail. Salespeople skip the second step of seeing the need from the customer's perspective or their conclusions are based on empiricism.

A simple example:

Car salesperson Joe determines that his prospects, Jason and Heather, a couple in their twenties with two young children, need a better car. Jason and Heather have narrowed their decision to a choice between two. The first is a minivan with basic features and the second is a much more expensive SUV with extra bells and whistles.

Joe has determined that Jason's salary would qualify him for a loan for either vehicle. Both vehicles would meet their transportation needs. But the SUV payments and insurance would push the couple's dream of owning a home, out of reach. Joe does not know they are thinking about buying a home.

Heather is perfectly happy with the minivan. Jason wants the SUV because of the four-wheel drive, higher profile, and stereo package that is on the vehicle. Joe has found Jason's hot buttons. Joe concentrates on filling the need of Jason's desire to drive a vehicle that more closely matches his testosterone level.

Joe applies the high-pressure tactics and the tension finally causes a sales explosion. Heather leaves the showroom to sit in their old car. Jason soon follows and they drive away. After a heated debate on the road, the couple spots another dealership. They stop there and decide to compromise. They purchase an extended cab pick up truck that costs much less than the four-wheel drive SUV.

Joe waited around for Jason and Heather to return long after his quitting time. He was sure he had them sold and they would *be back*.

Determining that people have a need and seeing it from their perspective does not alone produce empathy. Steps one and two give you the information or knowledge you need, Step three produces empathy. In our previous example, Joe skipped step two. If he had understood that Jason and Heather were budgeting to enable the purchase of a home, he might have stopped there and saw the house idea as an objection to his objective (to sell the more expensive vehicle and make more commission),

or

he could have used that information to remind himself of a time when he was younger with less money and how he felt when a slick salesperson got him to buy a pair of expensive jet skis and trailer on credit when he couldn't even afford a car to haul them. I'm sure invoking those emotions in Joe would have got him to persuade his prospects to look at the mini-van more closely or perhaps suggest a compromise. That's empathy in action. Then Joe would have made a sale.

I know there are plenty of skeptics that believe that this doesn't really work or that this process is too much work. They think that by concentrating on those 'hot buttons' without concern for the buyer's best interests is faster and will produce more sales. On any given day they just might. Even so, I have worked along side plenty of these salespeople and by practicing empathy have consistently *outsold them time and time again.*

And:

I have had far less rejections.

I have had less returns or buyer's remorse.

I have sold at higher profits.

I have provided better service.

I have had more referrals.

How does all of this help you get the job and pay you want?

When you are looking for a job:

You are the service or product.
The employer is the customer.
You are selling.
The employer is buying.

Use the steps to empathy in your interview. Then use them in your job and life. I ask you to please listen to this advice from a fellow earth inhabitant, take this chapter to heart. Become a student and practitioner of empathy. This will help you deal with people in every aspect of your life. The rewards are celestial.

◆———————————————◆

9. The Best Way I Found To Build My Confidence

The Third Step of LEAP

Assess if you can *and want* to meet their needs and desires.

Early in my career I arrived at an appointment for a consulting job on the first floor of a twenty-story building. An assistant had called stating that his boss was considering the acquisition of a business and would like my advice. When I asked the guard what floor the company was on that I was looking for she responded, "all twenty floors." I had no idea the company was that large, and did not even know what they did. She asked whom I was there to see and when I told her Mr. Gorman she directed me to an auditorium style meeting room on one of the upper floors.

The room had over seventy seats arranged in a half circle, covered in maroon crushed velvet facing a stage. I had just taken a seat when people began filing into the room. I was sure I had the wrong place when Mr. Gorman introduced himself and asked me to take a place on the stage with him.

Before I could utter a word, Mr. Gorman stood at the microphone and announced, "Today we have a top expert in business assessment who will be taking your questions regarding our project 'Community Outreach' and the acquisition of the twenty six satellite clinics. The audience applauded and as I took my place behind the podium they became a surreal ocean of people.

Everything was moving in slow motion and I felt like I had been standing there for a long time, as everyone's eyes were fixated upon me as if in anticipation of prodigious words of wisdom.

This was the first I had heard of this project and knew nothing about the acquisition. I had to think fast. I slowly cleared my throat and said something like this, "I am honored to be here before you today. I would like to know your questions and concerns about this project. Would you please raise your hand if you have something to say and I will listen to you one at a time."

For the next hour and a half I listened to questions and concerns while I took notes. During this period I had plenty of time to plot my exit. After listening to everyone speak, I muttered, "Thank you for your valuable questions and comments today. I will be contacting Mr. Gorman and return in two weeks with the proposal, which will answer all of your questions. I will begin work immediately." While the audience applauded, I quickly left out the side door. I ran past the elevator and to the stairwell. After descending almost twenty flights of stairs, I ran to my car and sped away. My heart was pounding and I felt like I had just made a great escape.

The project was complex and over my head. My intentions were to call Mr. Gorman the next day to tell him

I was not the man for the job, and toss the notes in the trash.

Later that evening I had dinner with a friend of mine, Tyson, who was much more experienced at mergers and acquisitions at the time, than I. I was sure the story was going to get some big laughs. He found the event amusing but instead of laughing asked if we could go over to my office and take a look at my notes. I obliged.

After studying the notes, Tyson asked me if I wanted to take on the job.

"I don't think I can," I responded.

He asked me a second question, "If you were confident that you could do this job, would you?"

"Yes." I answered without hesitation.

"Why?"

"Because I liked the people and I would welcome the opportunity for the challenge."

"Why did they call you?"

"Well, while I was fielding questions, one employee asked what I estimated the time frame would be for a proposal. She stated they had contacted several large firms and all of them told her a proposal would take three to four months, and they need one within thirty days."

"There you have it," he remarked.

"What do I have?"

"You have something they need the big guys don't have. You have speed, you can move fast. Look over these notes. For what this job is worth you can hire a couple of assistants, a tax expert, and a programmer to work for you. Sleep on it and call me tomorrow."

I was so anxious I couldn't sleep that night. I poured through my notes and began forming a plan. This would be the biggest consulting job I'd landed, and all because I had something the big guys didn't.

The next day I was on the phone looking for people with the right expertise. For five days I burned the candle at both ends until I had the people I needed, the costs estimated, and a completed proposal. I called Mr. Gorman and returned to meet with his staff and answered every question with confidence.

Until that day I had never charged more than half of what the big consulting firms charged. I was just a small guy. Yet I realized that if I had something those firms didn't have I should be charging as much or more. I bid that job at double my normal rate and Mr. Gorman signed my contract without a second thought. I learned an important lesson about value that day.

The project lasted almost a year and was a stupendous success. I had gone from running down a fire stairwell to finding equal footing with much larger competitors, all because I became a believer. *I became a believer by getting the knowledge I needed to prove that I could and wanted to do the job.* I learned that becoming a believer is the best way I know to become confident.

Remember that all of your contact with a prospective company, including telephone calls, email, mail, the interview, and investigative work is your opportunity to assess the company.

What is your first impression of them?

Do you want to work for them?

Is the salary enough to keep you interested?

If your gut feeling is still good then gather all of the information you have about the company and their needs and desires. Discover if you can meet those needs and desires.

The easiest way for you to convince anyone of anything is to first be convinced yourself.

When you know what they need and desire, then you can assess whether or not you can and want to serve that need and desire. If the answer is no, call and tell the employer and send a 'thanks but no thanks card.' Explain that after careful assessment you have reached your conclusion. A good employer will appreciate a considerate no thanks.

Persuading people to act in their best interests is noble.

10. The Seven A's of Persuasion

The Fourth Step of LEAP

Persuade your employer that you can *help them* meet those needs and desires better than anyone else on the planet.

During the time period when my eyesight was vitiating, I knew that selling skills were pertinent to acquiring and performing most jobs, so I read every sales book I could get my hands on. I conceived that should I lose my eyesight altogether, I could always use selling skills regardless of a lack of vision. When reading became so cumbersome that one book took weeks to complete, I started listening to books on tape. Many authors and motivational speakers mentioned persuasion. Persuasion was described as winning over through debate or reasoning, or convincing someone.

I needed more knowledge about persuasion. I had found the support for eliminating pretense in the first three steps of LEAP. I knew that no matter how good I became at the first three steps of LEAP, I would have to be even better at step four, '*Persuade.*'

When I had listened to a customer, developed empathy, and assessed the needs and desires, I believed in my cause. Now I needed to find the most powerful principles of persuasion and an easy to follow and remember plan. I picked up a dictionary and began searching for words that described the principles of persuasion. Quite commonly, I started with the letter 'A.' The first day I found seven words that perfectly represented the principles I was looking for.

In the following days, I continued my search through the alphabet encountering more descriptive vocabulary. I did not find any words that more distinctively represented the principles of persuasion than the original seven, all beginning with 'A.' I had what I was looking for.

I have used these seven principles throughout my life to accomplish amazing feats of persuasion. Here are the dynamic principles I have used for years to perfect my persuasion skills and attain astounding success:

The Seven A's of Persuasion

Announce

Arouse

Align

Affirm

Assure

Assist

Adjourn

Announce, Arouse, Align, Affirm,
Assure, Assist, Adjourn

Announce

Announce the direction.

Make sure people know the subject of your persuasion.

1. Announce their needs and desires to be sure you know and understand them. Let them know what you believe. When you are selling yourself, make sure they know what they are buying in relationship to what they need.

2. Announce that you can and want to fulfill your prospective employer's needs and desires.

Employer Secret 20: Just because you show up for the interview doesn't mean the employer knows you want the job. When I have asked employers why they did not hire a particular candidate one answer I have heard repeatedly is: "I wasn't sure they wanted the job."

Remember that you need to assess the job and determine if you *want* the job. If you want the job, make sure the interviewer knows it!

Arouse

Arouse within people the same emotions you get from the ideas that make you a believer.

Be enthusiastic and infectious. Instill your passion in others. This is not done in one simple step but as a principle that is practiced throughout all other principles and acts of persuasion. If you are not passionate about your career or the job you are applying for find a reason to become passionate or find a different career.

Align

Align your product with their need and desire.

When you know what skills the employer is looking for, make sure the employer knows you have them. When you know what issues the employer is facing, let the employer know how your skills are the solutions.

1. Align their interests with yours. Form an alliance with people. They should know you're in this together.

2. Align your behavior with your customer. Mirror their level of energy. Then to arouse them increase your level one step at a time. It's much easier to lead people up a flight of stairs one at a time than to attempt to drag them or see how high they can jump. Your energy level is portrayed in the volume level, inflection, and speed of your voice, and your words. Your energy level is portrayed in your body language, how you position yourself and your arms, feet, hands, and head and how fast you move. Your energy level is depicted in your eye movements, the speed, the eye-to-eye contact, and the direction you are looking.

Affirm

Affirm your customer's (prospective employer's)
beliefs and position.

One of the most amazing salespeople I ever met was a retired door-to-door salesman who was working part time selling motor homes. Henry worked only twenty hours per week and would quietly outsell every one of his associates toiling forty to sixty hours per week.

He had perfected the art of affirmation. He had learned to use affirmation when customers agreed and objected. He made positive statements convincingly and with enthusiasm.

Here are some examples of what he said when customers "saw the light" as he put it:

"That's right!"

"You're right!"

"You're one of the few people who get it."

"See!"

When customers discovered a feature of a motor home he made them feel like they invented it. He'd say:

"I thought no one would ever see that."

"Isn't that something?"

"You've found it."

When customers disagreed with him or objected he would still affirm their position by declaring:

"That's exactly what I used to think."

"I can see why you believe that."

"That is the same concern I had."

"That is a very good concern."

"I would be thinking the same thing as you."

"That is an excellent question."

"How observant. No one has ever asked that before."

And when customers purchased he stated:

"You've made such a good decision."

"I can't wait to get pictures from your first vacation."

"You are going to thank me again later."

Henry used to tell me, "If you want to convince anyone of anything let them know when they are already right."

These same skills can be used in 'job selling.' When an interviewer expresses a concern.

Example One:
Interviewer: "Seems like programmers are a dime a dozen."
Candidate: "That's exactly what I used to think. My last employer found that although there were large responses to her ads, good programmers with stable work histories were sparse."

Example Two:
Interviewer: "From your resume it appears that you were demoted from bank management to a teller position. Is that true?"
Candidate: "How observant. That's what I would have asked. The teller position was actually a Saturday only job in addition to my management position. I worked Saturdays as a teller to interact with customers in person."

Affirm customer's (employer's) beliefs and objections. Let them know when they get something right. Declare their position correct or affirm that you understand. Congratulate them and rejoice with them when they join you, and never be a sore loser when they do not.

Assure

Assure your customer's (prospective employer's) decisions.

Once there was a shortage of labor when I was hiring for a warehouse position. I needed help immediately yet I had only one applicant. John Dunn was a man who looked as he could do the job yet he could not read or write enough to complete an application. During the interview he told me how he had lost his father when he was a child and had to quit school to work on the family farm.

After the interview I was still hesitant about hiring him until he stood, shook my hand vigorously, stared me straight in the eye and announced, " I can do the job and I would be honored to work for you. I will make you proud to have hired me." He stated those words with such conviction that I can still hear him today. I did hire him and was proud I did.

John Dunn taught me that there is magic in assuring someone of what you believe. We all need assurance. I have learned to provide assurance throughout my selling.

I discovered that when I believe in my products or service, providing assurance is very easy. I began including comments of assurance throughout my sales presentations.

Not all assurance statements are positive. After listening to salespeople and job candidates for years, I have classified assurance statements into three types:

The Three Types of Assurance Statements
1. Negative Assurance Statements
2. Assumption Assurance Statements
3. Positive Assurance Statements

1. Negative Assurance Statements

Negative assurance statements attempt to reduce fear, but can instead induce fear. I have heard salespeople make the following statements to me when I've been the prospect:

"You won't be disappointed."
(Until this point I had not even considered that possibility. I was so excited about this new product that all I was thinking about is taking it home. I have been disappointed with products before, especially when making such spontaneous decisions – I'd better wait and think about this!)

"You won't have to worry about this car breaking down."
(I had not even considered that a new car would be breaking down. I was ready to buy, now I think I better read the warranty and maybe go home and check this car's dependability ratings.)

This is a conversation I had with a job candidate: "I see you have experience compiling year end statements for Fortune 500 companies," I stated.

"Yes and if you hire me, there won't be mistakes when accounts are reconciled." the candidate said.

I immediately began to wonder why a candidate of this caliber would be concerned or mention these types of mistakes. If you noticed I did not ask the candidate a question, and a nod or 'yes' response would have been affirming. I remained silent to get more information.

"That only happened when the computer systems were down and we were forced to finish manually," he added.

Negative assurance statements create suspicion and not assurance. I don't use negative assurance statements because I don't like the possibility of reminding people of actual past experiences or alerting their subconscious mind to situations they need to avoid.

2. Assumption Assurance Statements

I also avoid making *assumption* assurance statements. These statements are often positive assurance statements that are made prematurely. Numerous times while shopping alone I have heard a salesperson spout, "Your wife will love it!" I'm thinking, this character has not met my wife and has no idea what her tastes are.

While I was looking at a sunroom at a home show the salesman stated, "This siding will look perfect on your house." This guy assumed I was looking at the siding samples. I had a brick home.

Assumption assurance statements indicate selfishness or laziness. They say I don't really care about your needs and desires.

Frequently, assumption assurance statements involve items of personal preference such as color. "You'll love the hunter green." This statement really says, "Your preferences are not important to me, I am only concerned that the decision is made."

While interviewing a lady for a management position within two minutes of our introduction and before I had even described the position, she made this statement:

"I am certain that I'm perfect for your position."

These types of statements are red flags. They are red flags for selling, 'job selling,' and dating. I avoid making assumption assurance statements at all costs. Making these comments blow a hole in credibility that is almost impossible to climb out of.

By practicing the first three steps of LEAP, I am educated enough about my customer's needs and desires to make positive assurance statements, not assumption assurance statements.

3. Positive Assurance Statements

A statement of assurance should reinforce a concept or belief. Here are some I have used:

> *My door will always be open for you.*
> *Our service department stands ready to serve you.*
> *I'll make sure that is done.*
> *I use this product, I love this product, and this product has been terrific for me.*

I want you to have the same fabulous experience I have had.

HINT: I have learned that most positive assurance statements are about my company, my service, my product, or myself, that assures my customer's needs and desires. I find I cannot assure anything that is not within my power or best faith.

Remembering to provide *assurance* is paramount and why this is one of the 'Seven A's of Persuasion."

Consistently assure people that everything will be all right and that they are doing the right thing, with the same reasons you believe they are doing the right thing. After completing the other three steps of LEAP, you will have the confidence of knowing these are the right reasons.

Employers want assurance. Assurance is what employers are looking for when they check references. Using the testimony of others helps provide assurance.

Assist
Assist the action needed.

Be ready to help people take the steps to complete their decisions and then assist them. If they need to sign a contract - have a pen. If they need to make a call – offer your telephone. I have even called an employer where I applied and scheduled my own interview. *Take the initiative and help them make decisions!*

<u>A</u>djourn

Adjourn your effort at the right time.

One of the biggest mistakes I have seen many candidates and salespeople make is overselling. This mistake is big because the salesperson has usually done most of the work and then tears the sale apart. When the customer is sold and the salesperson keeps selling, what happens is:

The customer becomes suspect because the salesperson has stopped focusing on the customer.

KNOW WHEN TO STOP.

If an interviewer gives you sold signs, STOP SELLING. Sold signs like: How soon can you start? Or: We'd like to make you an offer.

The word adjourn means postpone or stop until next time. This word well defines the meaning of the last principle of persuasion. Stop selling when your prospective employer is sold. However, this does not mean you are done selling forever. You might need to sell again at the next objection, the next meeting, on the phone, during negotiation, or on the job.

How have these principles helped me? Practicing LEAP and the Seven A's of Persuasion have got me the jobs I've wanted, helped me become a top salesperson and succeed in business. Once when I was applying for a sales job the interviewer told me, "Your references had great things to say about you. One even said that you were the best salesperson he has ever worked with and that you could sell refrigerators to Eskimos. So describe to me how you would sell refrigerators to Eskimos." (Including references with my resume got me into this jam. I never included references when sending my resume again and would suggest you not provide references with your resume either.)

After a brief pause I answered him. "Eskimos live in an extremely cold climate, where temperatures are often far below the inside of the average refrigerator. I would explain to the Eskimos how a refrigerator could keep their food from freezing and still cold enough to be safe. The refrigerator would eliminate thawing of cold foods and reduce the cooking time of prepared meals."

The interviewer was impressed.

As I am usually not so quick on my feet, I attribute the answer to LEAP. I simply listened to the question, and empathized with the customer by imagining myself as an Eskimo, which allowed me to assess the need, to persuade the Eskimos.

Remember this:
Honest persuasion can only come from a believer.
Persuasion from any less position is perversion
(wrongly self-willed).

THE FOUR SIMPLE STEPS OF SELLING
To Get From Self Focus to Customer Focus Just...
LEAP

Learn

Empathize

Assess

Persuade

Learn *who* your employer is.
Learn your employer's needs and desires.
Use the <u>'Nine Lessons of Listening Science'</u>
Lessons One, Two, and Three
Shut up
Listening Science Lesson Four
Ask Questions
Listening Science Lesson Five
Ask pertinent questions.
Listening Science Lesson Six
Relate to Them
Listening Science Lesson Seven
Be Interested
Listening Science Lesson Eight
Remember What They've Said
Listening Science Lesson Nine
Timing is critical.

'The Three Steps to Effective Empathy'
1. Determine if the other person has a need or desire.
2. See other peoples' needs or desires *from their perspective or best interests.* This is informed empathy and is critical.
3. Relate their need or desire with the closest need or desire of your own in order to *invoke the same or similar feelings within yourself.*

Assess if you can *and want* to meet their needs and desires.

The Seven A's of Persuasion
Announce Arouse Align Affirm,
Assure Assist Adjourn

▼▼▼▼▼▼▼▼▼▼▼▼▼▼▼▼▼▼▼▼▼▼▼▼▼▼▼▼▼▼▼▼`

III. The Secrets of the Hunt

If you are not at least well informed about yourself, how can anyone expect you to be knowledgeable about any other subject?

11. How You Can Avoid the Number One Way Applicants are Ruled Out

Once I worked for a supply company that delivered material to construction sites. I was in charge of hiring drivers for a fleet of trucks. We were always hiring as the company was experiencing growth and there was constant turnover. Subsequently we would even accept temporary employees.

Applicants for these positions came from all walks of life. They were accountants, teachers, newspaper reporters, managers, salespeople, and more. Anyone who was literate with a valid driver's license was qualified.

We screened candidates by job application. We would eliminate candidate after candidate just by the application.

In addition to the record keeping that was required, I had created my own tracking register of the information supplied by these job candidates. After inspecting one thousand applications, I was astounded by theses applicants' inability to correctly complete a simple job application. The next page shows my results:

11. How You Can Avoid the Number One Way Applicants are Ruled Out

Completed Applications

Out of 1000

Incorrect Date	212
Incorrect Year	77
Misspelled Own Name	34
Incomplete Address	191
Incorrect Address	112
Wrong Telephone Number	178
More than 3 questions left blank	578
More than 5 questions left blank	394
Previous Convictions/Did not check yes or no	227
Did not sign application	112
Did not enter any past experience	165
Did not have complete reference information	516

Out of the first five blanks on the application, over twenty per cent did not know the date, over seven percent wrote down the incorrect year, nineteen percent did not give a complete address, over seventeen percent wrote the wrong telephone number, and three percent actually misspelled their own name!

I was shocked at how many people would disqualify themselves by not being able give an employer their correct telephone number.

At that time our applications requested a candidate's height and weight. I have received applications from people that stated they were twelve inches tall and weighed only ten pounds. One candidate listed his weight in ounces. I have met people that claim to have attended college for two hundred years and have been in their last job for eighty.

Anyone who has not experienced truth that is stranger than fiction should read job applications. I have actually seen the following answers on applications:

Please list your past experience:

> *I don't believe in reincarnation.*
> *I like to live in the present.*
> *Available upon my request.*
> *Did not keep track.*
> *I have no experience but I am willing to find some.*

And two of my favorites:

> *I have no past.*
> *I'm not married.*

Under please list references I have seen:

> *Dictionary, Almanac, and the Guinness Book of World Records*

Over the years I have seen just as inadequate and ridiculous answers on applications from accountants, attorneys, bankers, brokers, chemists, college professors, doctors, managers, news announcers, pilots, and more. No level of education or position is immune to the blunders and lack of ability for completing a job application.

Surveys have reported and as you can see from my records, *by far the number one application deficiency is the omission of information.* In spite of some candidates' purposeful omission of information, leaving questions blank is largely due to the candidate's inadequate preparation.

After examining so many applications, one day I put my team and myself to the test. You should have seen the looks I got when I requested everyone in the office complete a job application within thirty minutes. This was more than adequate time to complete our two-page application. These folks were used to my creative and sometimes harebrain ideas so when I mentioned that the project was for research, they went right to work.

My experiment revealed that no one had completed all of the questions or blanks. I was the worst offender with twenty-one bits of information missing. There was no way I could remember all of my information. The best application was still missing twelve items. Granted we were not prepared, but if the people doing the hiring could not even complete the job application, how could we expect the candidates to?

The next time I became a job seeker, I knew that in order to fill out a job application, I needed help.

The only way I could correctly and completely fill out a job application was if I had all of the information in front me. Since I do not have a photographic memory and could not recall all the schools' addresses I had attended, my exact dates of employment history, reference's addresses and telephone numbers, and the rest, I had to find a way to organize all of this information.

My lack of eyesight made searching for papers around the house or office a frustrating and time consuming chore. I needed an easy way to keep this personal data altogether and remember to always bring these papers with me to an interview or to apply for a job.

Even as a boy I was always forgetting something when leaving the house. My mother used to tell me; "If your head wasn't attached to your body you would forget your self."

That is how I named my personal data package, my 'SELF.' Then I only had to remember to bring my 'SELF' to job interviews.

SELF

Schooling

Experience

Lists

Forms

I categorized **SELF** as follows:

Schooling

- Name
- Address
- Phone
- Dates Attended
- Awards
- Studies
- Degrees
- Grade Point Average

Experience

- Company Name
- Supervisor's Name
- Address
- Phone
- Dates Employed
- Job Title
- Reason for Leaving
- Equipment Operated
- Office Equipment Operated

- Software Experience
- Specific Technical Skills

Lists

Personal

- Birth date
- Social Security Number
- Address
- Telephone Number

References

- Names
- Addresses
- Phone Numbers
- Occupations

Forms

- Professional Licenses
- Military Discharge Papers
- Driver's License or Photo Identification Copy
- Social Security Card Copy
- Visa or Work Papers
- Resume
- Special Certification Copies

I typed the information in a large, easy to read font, on several sheets of paper. I later reduced this to a few four by six inch cards with my forms and included two sharpened pencils and a pen in a nine by twelve inch envelope, marked SELF. Even though I have not been a job seeker for a considerable number of years, I still have that envelope!

This information and anything else you need when going to an interview or apply for a job is critical. This data is confidential and should be kept in a safe place. Keep this file updated at least once a year and you'll always be prepared. *Being prepared generates confidence.*

Always bring several copies of your resume with your 'SELF' to an interview. If the interview begins and you do not see a copy of your resume present, slide one across the desk or table to the interviewer at an opportune moment.

Employer Secret 114: Sometimes the individual that is interviewing you is reading your resume for the first time.

Employer Secret 122: The person interviewing you might not have a copy of your resume.

Employer Secret 112: Sometimes the individual that is interviewing you has not even seen your resume.

These situations could happen because:
1. The person interviewing you is not the same as the person who originally saw your cover letter and resume.
2. Sometimes, between the time your interview was scheduled and your interview, your resume has been misplaced.
3. Sometimes the decision to schedule your interview was based solely on the merit of your cover letter.

I typically sat across from candidates with a copy of their resume in front of me. I would quietly read and refer to their resume and base my questions from this information. Hardly ever did a candidate have the resume memorized.

I asked candidates to recite their objective to me. More than half did not even come close and almost none could recite verbatim. Candidates were unsure of the chronological order of their work history on their resumes. When I based questions on the resume statements about their skills and job descriptions, dumbfounded looks were not uncommon. Apparently, more than a few had not written their own resumes and I don't think some had ever read them. Hiring someone to write a resume is fine, as long as they do not misinterpret or fabricate the facts.

Quite by accident (or necessity), I discovered a great trick for candidates and interviewers. Whenever I had interviews scheduled late in the day and my eye was fatigued, I could no longer read a resume. I frequently handed candidates a copy of their epitome and asked them to read certain sections aloud, one at a time, while I followed along. Resumes came alive. Candidates were more relaxed and confident. When I had them look at their own resume while I asked questions, they became more at ease and demonstrated more trust.

Hint: Keep a copy of your resume in front of *yourself* during the interview.

There may be additional people brought in to meet you such as a department head or the position supervisor. If anyone requests a copy of your resume from the interviewer, you'll look prepared when you have extra copies.

CAUTION: Be especially aware of the demeanor or comments from the interviewer before you hand out resumes to others. I have known some HR personnel that heavily guard their power and refuse to provide resumes to any other departments or company managers.

After years of experience and research I have discovered that for employers using applications, not only is the number one application deficiency the omission of information, this is often the *first consideration when disqualifying candidates*, and the *number one reason for elimination.*

The previous one sentence should be enough reason for every single person whoever needs to seek employment to create a 'SELF' file or order a 'SELF File Kit' *right now.*

To make keeping your self together *easy*, visit www.employersecrets.com for more information on a 'SELF File Kit.'

Bring your SELF when you go to apply for a job.

◆————————————◆

When one person provides two contending answers to the same question of fact, even if both are correct, the respondent comes under suspicion.

12. The Employer's Secret Lie Detector

Employers will match application information against your resume. I have heard candidate's say, "You have my resume, why do you need me to fill out this application?" or "Can I skip the job history and just note - please see resume?' Most employers will want your job history and all other facts completed. Whether the application is a boilerplate or customized form, the candidate is usually required to sign the document attesting that all answers are true and correct.

The best way to ensure your application information is consistent with your resume is to *bring your resume to the interview* in your 'SELF' file.

Employer Secret 52: Job applications are effective lie detectors.

At our company, job candidates are required to complete applications at our office before the interview. The application is handed to the candidate upon arrival. Most candidates feel pressure to complete the application within a reasonable period of time.

Ten Ways an Application can be a Lie Detector Before A Background Check

1. The education dates do not correspond with the birth date. Ten year olds seldom graduate from college.
2. Education dates do not conform to dates of employment or home addresses.
3. The telephone prefix does not correspond with home or work address. Cell phone numbers can rule this one out.
4. Time at home addresses does not correspond with employment dates. Example: Time at present residence is two years, yet work experience shows the last job was located on the opposite coast and the termination date was six months ago.
5. The work history is not in harmony with the resume.
6. Degree is not offered at listed educational institution.
7. Time spent in school does not conform to degree.
8. Technical or professional skills claimed could not derive from education or experience listed.
9. Work history is questionable based on education. People have lied about difficult to verify experience to meet job description qualifications.
10. Military service dates conflict with employment or education time periods.

Some of these are not lies, just innocent errors. Employers will not take the time to distinguish between the two and most always will not accept lies or errors.

You can usually not afford even one mistake
during the hiring process.

13. Why I Never Answer the Phone

When my company had only four people I used to want to answer every call that came in to our business and I tried to do just that. As the owner and a salesperson, I am one of the most knowledgeable about our business and services and wanted to talk to every prospect that called. I wanted to strike when the iron was hot, after all if they didn't get their issue resolved during that call to our business, they would probably call our competitor next.

While that might generally be an ideal situation, there was an unexpected negative repercussion that had the potential to cause me considerable damage more than once. I would be in the middle of a time sensitive project with a blanket of papers covering my desk, performing complex spreadsheet calculations, when a call would come.

One particular afternoon I was working on an appraisal that had to be ready for a court case the next day. I answered the phone and the caller was an important client. I was selling his business and had been negotiating with the buyer. He informed me that a crisis with a supplier had been resolved with new, lower pricing, a key employee agreed to a pay cut but was still out on the vacation issue, and there had been a mistake on the present value of the business because his accountant had included over one million dollars in assets that were previously sold. He stated that he was resigned to the deal and wanted to work with the buyer. Two more lines were ringing so I hurriedly made notes and took another call.

The buyer for his business called while I was on another line. My new office manager, Jane, let me know that the buyer was waiting for me. I gave her the notes and requested she relay the information to the buyer. Here are my notes:

crisis with a supplier - over - lower pricing
key employee cut OK - out on vacation
mistake on assets - sold
owner is resigned

Here is what Jane interpreted from my notes and communicated to the buyer:

There was a crisis with a supplier over lower pricing, a key employee had been cut and would be out on vacation, the business assets have been mistakenly sold, and the owner has resigned.

She told me the buyer was silent for several seconds, then just said "goodbye," and hung up.

I was devastated. This was entirely my fault. I usually never ask anyone to communicate information in an important negotiation. I had not been focusing. While eating humble pie and enduring several tense conversations, I barely salvaged the deal.

Another time, when I was having multiple conversations, I bought over one hundred fluorescent light bulbs from an industrious telemarketer. (Our office had no fluorescent lights.)

The most important calls always came at the least opportune times. My telecommunications were out of control. I had to make a change.

I made only one. *I stopped answering all of my phones.*

I blocked out entire mornings and afternoons during my workdays when I would not take calls. I set aside times at several intervals during the day when I would return calls. I had people to answer the phone, voice mail, and caller ID to identify emergencies.

My personal and business life changed dramatically. Suddenly there seemed to be four more hours in a day, a whole extra day every week. My initial concern was that I would spend more time playing 'phone tag.'

What happened next more than compensated for any extra calls. When people left me messages they frequently told me what they wanted. I was prepared and a step ahead when I returned their calls and sometimes I found the information they left did not warrant a return call and saved more time. I shut my office door during important conversations and my environment was quiet and controlled.

I was able to completely focus on the tasks at hand without interruption. My productivity increased and revenue grew by over one hundred per cent the very next quarter.

When I call candidates they are often caught off guard. They are distracted and often make an undesirable impression. People are very busy and with cell phones they can be anywhere at anytime. Waiting all day to hear if you got the interview and then asking the employer if you can call them back because you are in a busy place and cannot hear or are driving does not make much sense. The employer might feel that you are not taking the opportunity seriously if you answer and then have to call back.

People also respond differently when caught 'off guard' on the phone. Telemarketers relied on this fact for years.

Employer Secret 72: Some employers even use this 'off guard' technique during negotiations.

I worked with one HR manager that insisted all negotiation calls be made between six and seven p.m. He believed candidates were more pliable when pulled away from the dinner table.

People do not easily ignore silence on the phone. People make decisions faster on the phone. One of the mistakes of negotiating is responding too quickly. You can usually not *afford even one mistake* in the hiring process.

After spending a good deal of time talking on the telephone, if you are aware, you can sense if the person on the other end is sitting or standing, alone or with someone, smoking, busy, paying attention, sitting in front of a computer, driving, in a restaurant, smiling, or in a hurry.

Employer Secret 68: Employers are judging you on the telephone.

Top Ten
Telephone Mistakes

1. Calling or talking from a busy location such as a restaurant.
2. Not having voice mail or an answering machine.
3. Having an unprofessional voice mail greeting.
4. Talking too much.
5. Not listening and not taking notes.
6. Answering the phone (being caught off guard).
7. Leaving a telephone number where someone answers who is incapable of taking a message or volunteers irrelevant or inappropriate information.
8. Putting the caller on hold.
9. Asking inappropriate, irrelevant, or poorly timed questions.
10. Not returning calls promptly.

One powerful way to take control of your time and telephone conversations is to stop answering the phone. Set aside certain times each day to check messages and return calls. Return important calls promptly. Plan each call. If possible, stand and smile while talking on the phone.

14. The Secrets of Your Background Investigation

A booming carpet cleaner was growing faster than he could hire an experienced work force. In an interview the business owner was quoted as saying, "after several lean years, this is a good problem to have." The company quickly hired a dozen new employees.

One particular employee had claimed several years of experience and was sent out alone on several occasions. Unfortunately this was not the only lie on his application.

After only a short time working he was sent to a job where the female homeowner was present. After committing a violent attack, he was arrested and convicted of a felony. The employer discovered at the trial this was the defendant's second such conviction in ten years.

Negligence was alleged against the employer's hiring practices for failing to search criminal records. The employer spent so much money in defense that he is no longer in business.

Employers today have legitimate reasons to worry about who they are hiring. Although there were a number of challenges when hiring a new computer at Company YOU back in Chapter Two, there are even more concerns for the employer in the real world. Employers' interview questions are limited regarding a host of subjects including the use of drugs and alcohol.

Yet employers have become increasingly liable for the actions of their employees. Violence in the workplace, white-collar criminal activity including embezzlement, dishonesty, theft, violation of the information privacy law against clients and other employees, sexual harassment, and negligence are just some of these actions. Employees who commit these acts cost employers billions of dollars each year.

In order to protect themselves, employers have spent a substantial deal of time and money to develop and use elaborate screening procedures, psychological assessments, polygraph tests, background checks, and interview techniques.

Employer Secret 66: Employers and hiring agencies are aware that in certain states, laws provide legal immunity to former employers who divulge information to prospective employers.

You can be sure they will make your former employers aware of this when they check your references.

Employer Secret 64: Employers check credit scores.

The employer might request or conduct a credit check. Unless you are applying for a position at a bank, operating a cash register, or in security, this might not seem relevant. However, employers have several reasons to examine your credit report.

Why? One reason is to determine if the candidate is responsible. After all, if the computer you are considering at Company YOU cannot perform math functions, keep the current date, or track bills; is it really the computer for you? Some positions require the employee to handle cash or be responsible for transactions. Most businesses do not want an employee with financial issues in charge of their money.

Another reason is to confirm resume criteria such as employers and addresses or verify your stability.

For legal and insurance reasons the employer always wants to minimize their liability. When something goes wrong, the question will be; Did they do everything in their power to prevent such an occurrence when hiring?

Anyone could experience circumstances that cause credit trouble. We all need to make every effort to maintain good credit. Regarding your report - *just be aware of what's there.*

You will work way too hard to get interviews for a blurb of information floating around somewhere to rule you out without you even knowing it.

What are employers going to find out about you from a background check, credit report, or previous employer? You should know. Even if there is erroneous information being reported about you, *you should make sure you know first.* Get a copy of your report before the interview.

What can they do? A potential employer is required to notify you in writing and obtain your written permission if they are conducting a background check that involves your credit report. Employers cannot turn you down for a job because you filed bankruptcy.

Employer Secret 70: Not all employers follow this rule. There are now endless ways to obtain information about anyone without their knowledge via the Internet.

In addition, if you are not hired because of any information they obtain about you, they are required to provide you with the information so that you may challenge it. However, chances are if they obtained the information illegally, they are not going to inform you of what they found.

Obviously attempting to conduct a complete search to obtain all of the information about yourself on the Internet is probably not practical, but you can certainly check the major sources.

<u>What is the *best way* to pass a background check?</u>
Have a clean background and be aware of what information is out there about you, and *tell the truth*.

Your education is easy to verify. Arrest records are mostly public. Professional screening firms now check for felony and misdemeanor records. In addition to state records, many will check county records. Liability issues have bred weary employers who will no doubt provide only limited information about your past employment (unless you reside in one of the states that apply from Employer Secret 66 on page 128). Dates of employment, title, and job duties might be all they will verify.

Employer Secret 55: Candidates' confessions of past actions or admissions of flaws do not demonstrate honesty.

Don't Confess

You don't need to provide extra information that is not pertinent or requested.

Don't Make Excuses

If any true, yet undesirable, information about you should be revealed to you, don't make excuses. Simply accept the fact, own it and move on. If the employer wants to make an issue of this, keep job hunting.

Employer Secret 54: In many businesses, employers do not like to see that candidates have relocated between states more than once in the last seven years.

As most information databases are still state and county restrictive, candidates with multiple state addresses complicate background checks. As employers now outsource employment screening, the cost of investigating a candidate who has lived in four states in the last seven years can cost four times as much as a candidate who has lived in one state for the same time period.

Turnaround time for outsourced background checks can be two to five days. In house investigations can take two weeks. The better the quantity and accuracy of information provided by the candidate the more expedient the process will be.

Employer Secret 13: Employers set up blind PO boxes or email addresses and hide their identity in order to find out if their own employees are looking for work and what is on their resumes. They also do this to find out if their competitor's employees are job hunting. (A blind PO box ad is a help wanted ad with no company name and only a 'Post Office Box' address, or a blind email address.)

CAUTION: I would never send my resume to a blind PO box. Recruiting firms have been known to set up blind PO boxes to form target market lists. They contact responders with promises of interviews, for a price.

I know a resume firm that solicits business this way. They contact the responder to critique the resume, and then offer to *fix it* for a price.

In addition, there are people who place blind PO box ads to gather personal information for illegal purposes.

Even though a company might set up a blind PO box because they do not want their own employees or competitors to know they are hiring, I would not respond.

Employer Secret 93: If you are being considered for an interview, many employers will search online resume postings for your resume and then compare what you have sent them with what you have posted.

Employer Secret 94: Employers search online resume postings to see if their own employees are looking for another job.

Section IV Summary

Avoid the number one application deficiency;
The omission of information
This is often the first consideration when disqualifying
candidates, and the number one reason for elimination.

Always bring your 'SELF' when you apply for a job.
Make sure your application matches your resume.

One powerful way to take control of your time and
telephone conversations is to stop answering the phone. Set
aside certain times each day to check messages and return
calls.

Be aware of the best way to pass a background check
and know the second best way to pass a background check.
Beware of blind PO boxes.

For more information on background
investigations visit: www.employersecrets.com

▼▼▼▼▼▼▼▼▼▼▼▼▼▼▼▼▼▼▼▼▼▼▼▼▼▼▼▼▼▼▼▼

I know of one company that requires Human Resource personnel to complete one hundred practice interviews and observe fifty actual interviews before meeting even one job candidate.

IV. INTERVIEW TACTICS

You are identified before you are known.

15. The Most Important Five Minutes of Your Career

Numerous surveys have shown and my personal experience verifies, that the *majority* of interviewers have made a positive or negative decision about a candidate in the first five minutes of an interview. The interviewers have stated that when they have a negative feeling about the candidate, the applicant rarely if ever, overcomes this impression during the rest of the interview. The interviewers also state that when they feel favorable about a candidate in those first five minutes, those people will move on to the next phase of the hiring process unless they disqualify themselves in some way, such as admitting unacceptable behavior in the past, or committing some radical blunder. The interviewers further say they usually spend no additional time looking at those candidates' cover letters and resumes.

Since the majority of hiring decisions are influenced in the first five minutes of a job interview, these five minutes become *the most important five minutes of your career.*

Obviously, there have been only a few questions asked and answered in the majority of interviews in the first five minutes. In fact, in the common scenario, the interviewer has done the greatest amount of talking during that time period.

So what is it in the first five minutes of an interview that is so powerful to cause an interviewer to form such a strong opinion about you?

YOUR FLAG!

When ships were sailing the oceans years before modern communication technology, the initial contact between vessels was the first visible part of any ship. Due to the unobstructed view on the open sea and curvature of the earth, this point was the top of the highest mast. Because of this, allies and enemies alike began flying their flags from atop their highest mast. *Ships were identified as friend or foe before the ships themselves were visible.*

This is exactly what's happening in the first five minutes of the interview. You are being identified from your flag as friend or foe, long before the interviewer has seen your ship or knows your course.

What is your FLAG? Your F.L.A.G.™ represents the most probable and likely the only possible factors from which the interviewer has had the opportunity to make any personal judgment.

Your FLAG is:

F First Words

L Listening Ability

A Attitude and Appearance

G Genuineness (in your voice and body language)

Fly Your Flag!

The average candidate spends several hundred hours looking for a job, including creating resumes, writing cover letters, scanning the ads, sending resumes, networking, and going to interviews. I am willing to bet the average job applicant spends considerably more time on any one of these single 'job searching' activities than on what will happen in the first five minutes of an interview.

Sure you need a great resume and cover letter and a place to send them to even get an interview, but if the first five minutes of an interview are the most important, how can you prepare? You can use the few simple following steps I have outlined for 'FLAG.'

First Words

Your first words include your language (the words you use), your timing, and your voice inflection.

Your language can demonstrate your level of intelligence, ability to relate, and grasp of the current situation. Speak clearly in complete sentences with proper English.

Do not immediately use acronyms, jargons, or above average vocabulary. The person interviewing you might not be as knowledgeable as you about your profession. Impressing someone is not about intimidating them. You can talk intelligently without intimidating your customer.

Maybe as or even more important than what you are saying is how you are talking. Your timing can show your level of anxiety or confidence, and patience. Are you calm? Are you commenting only at the appropriate moments? Are you interrupting? Don't answer questions abruptly. Take your time.

Your voice inflection can reveal your level of anxiety or confidence. Do you hesitate and clear your throat often?

Take a quick sales lesson from the pros. Be a chameleon. Match the 'energy level' of your interviewer. Mirror your interviewer's voice volume and speed as closely as you can. Talking faster or much louder than your interviewers can drain them of energy.

I once interviewed a young lady who spoke so fast I was exhausted from trying to keep up with just listening. After several attempts to slow her down I was forced to cut the interview short.

Talking much slower than the interviewer can make you appear unenthusiastic or tired.

Practice listening to others that you are engaged in conversation with and measure their speed to help you become aware of conversation tempo. Try mirroring their speech speed and volume.

Listening Ability

Remember the first step of 'LEAP'?

Learn your customer's needs and desires.

What is usually happening in the first five minutes of most job interviews, gives you this opportunity. The interviewer is usually describing the company and the position. They want to break the ice and gauge your level of interest. Sometimes the interviewer might be asking you questions, but you can be learning even by the questions he or she is asking.

Remember Step two of 'LEAP'?

Empathize with their position.

By practicing the first and second step of the 'LEAP' job selling skills, you will be demonstrating your listening ability, your attitude, and genuineness.

Attitude and Appearance

Your appearance is the first thing people see. With as much information as there is available on the subject, dressing and grooming yourself appropriately should be only as elusive as that last sentence is witty. If possible visit the company as mentioned earlier to observe the people coming and going. Dress at least *better* than how the present employees are garbed.

After seeing a myriad of job candidates from all walks of life, I can say that many practice poor hygiene and at the other end of the spectrum, some wear too much perfume or cologne. No employer wants employees with poor hygiene or overpowering odors in the work environment. Practice superb hygiene, do not wear perfumes or colognes unless needed, and then as little as possible. Some people have ultra sensitive smell. What might smell good to one person might make another ill.

Your body language is the second most important element of your appearance. Your body language makes a statement.

What you want to say is "I am confident, professional, and relaxed."

If you have not practiced the art of body language, here are a few interview tips:

- If at a table, keep your hands folded and in sight. Placing and folding your hands on the table is acceptable.
- If you hold a piece of paper, such as a resume don't move and wave the paper around until the pressed pulp becomes the center of attention.
- Move your body, hands, and limbs, at the same speed as the interviewer. When you stand, rise with the interviewer at the same speed.
- When in doubt, mirror the interviewer as much as possible.
- When interviewers were polled and asked what single gesture of body language designates a good attitude the number one answer was a smile.

I was once hired to perform in a training video for employers on interviewing. After the editing was completed I went in to take a look. As this had been a group project there was an audience of over a dozen people watching the film. I arrived a few minutes late and found a seat in the back. On the screen I was doing a good job speaking and using hand gestures at the appropriate times. Then I heard two women talking in front of me.

"He looks like he's on his way to the dentist," one whispered.

"No a funeral," the other chuckled.

I was embarrassed red nevertheless they were right. I was not smiling, and in fact looked like I was frowning. I sat through the remaining film, transfixed like I was seeing a train accident.

I decided right then I would change my appearance and learn to smile. The best way I discovered to do this was to practice talking in front of a mirror and smiling. (I found that when a person stands alone in a bathroom staring into the mirror talking to one's self, it's hard not to smile.)

When one of my clients had experienced double-digit growth for five straight years, supplying professional temporary workers for an industry that was in a tight market, I wanted to know her secret. Several of her competitors had gone under while she prospered.

I scheduled a lunch appointment and asked about her success. Here is what she told me:

"I contribute my success to keeping a daily eye on my cash flow, and hiring the right people. When applicants arrive at our office, the receptionist Mary, greets each one and provides them with a clipboard and application. Mary is a positive lady who is always smiling and making everyone feel welcome, exactly what a receptionist should do.

The applicants cannot see me, yet I can see and hear them from my desk. People will act differently with a receptionist than they will with an interviewer. Commonly, people see the receptionist as an instant comrade. After all, this person is usually friendly and seemingly alone and alienated, almost abandoned by the company. She often sits behind a counter like a bartender. Candidates will ask questions, tell stories, and confess sins to a receptionist.

When I conduct interviews I have people fill out an application and make sure I have scheduled at least twenty minutes at my desk to listen and watch each one before calling them back to the conference room. I have learned more about candidates in these twenty minutes than in many interviews.

Several times I have even posed as the receptionist. You can imagine their shock when I announce that I am ready to interview them. Some have confessed so much to me by that point they excuse themselves and practically run to their cars.

Mary and I have heard stories from how they were fired from their last job to personal stories about their spouses. We have both been asked an endless list of inappropriate questions about pay, benefits, other employees, the boss, and our personal lives. We have been asked on a date more than once."

A word of CAUTION: Receptionists, office managers, interviewers, and other employees of the business where you are applying will repeat anything you say. No matter how friendly a receptionist is, a candidate should not expect or attempt to form an alliance in order to gather information. This is *not* how to spy on the employer.

Employer Secret 28: Employers do watch or 'spy' on candidates every moment during their visit.

Employer Secret 10: Some employers have hidden disqualifiers.

One business owner told me he has the receptionist place an X on any application when the applicant does not have a pencil or a pen. Even if the interview is still conducted, this X eliminates the applicant from consideration.

Many employers will not hire anyone who is even one minute late for an interview no matter what the excuse. After all, if a man or woman cannot be punctual for the interview how will they show up on time for work?

I presume the way candidates conduct themselves in an interview will be the best behavior I will ever see from them. This is why even the smallest hint of bad manners will rule out a candidate.

We've all heard *"be on your best behavior."* What exactly is your best behavior? When was the last time you were on your best behavior? Many people answer 'at a wedding.' (Probably not referring to the reception.) What you should be is *'beyond your best behavior.'*

Genuineness

Listening and practicing true empathy produces genuineness.

Smile genuinely. Do not offer false flattery.

16. The Secrets of Interview Questions

I conducted a business class of HR personnel and the average number of interviews conducted per attendee in the room was over one thousand. Notwithstanding, there are smaller companies where the interviewer wears varying hats, with today's employment and hiring laws, employers are usually well rehearsed. The point is the person across the table from you is probably more experienced at interviewing than you are at being interviewed.

Most job candidates have been to less than twenty-five interviews in their life. Do the math. You have got to practice your sales presentation. If you don't have your sales presentation down to a science, you are going to be eaten alive!

This does not mean you memorize answers to every possible question. A sales presentation is not about rehearsing answers to every specific question. You will need to practice and prepare, but a sales presentation is about *determining and assessing* your customer's needs, and being sure yourself, first, and then convincing them that you will best fill those needs.

One way to recognize what the customer's needs are is to identify the question types the interviewer is asking.

Employer Secret 75: Employers use tactically planned questions based on the information they are looking for.

There are several general question category types used by employers that can be classified as follows:

- Past behavioral questions
- Future situation questions
- Knowledge and Experience questions
- Verified Questions
- Verifiable Questions
- Fishing Questions

Employer Secret 73: Employers often use a point scale to rate your answers.

Past Behavioral Questions

The idea behind these types of questions is that a person's past behavior predicts their future actions. Employers take significant stock in these answers.

Our entire credit system is founded on this principal. People and businesses are loaned money based on how they have paid their bills in the past.

Our judicial system relies on this principal. People with convictions for past criminal behavior are dealt with more harshly than first time offenders.

You need to be prepared to present your past in an honest and positive manner.

Examples of past behavioral questions:

Can you tell me about a time when you had to choose between honesty and dishonesty and how you made your decision?

Can you tell me about a past situation where you found a creative solution to a tough problem?

Can you tell me about a time when you had a problem employee, what the specific problem was, and how you handled it? (Management position)

Answers to past behavioral questions theoretically predict future job performance if the answers are accurate. Follow up questions to the candidate are aimed at measuring the validity of the answer. The candidate might be asked to provide a supervisor's name that can collaborate the answers. Or the interviewer might ask follow up 'trip' questions to establish validity, such as:

Can you tell me what year and month that happened and at which job?

This question implies that the company might be validating this information in some way and the candidate could suddenly feel a bit of uneasiness, especially if the answer was difficult to recall or deviated from the truth.

More questions such as these might follow:

Can you tell me how the employee reacted?

Can you tell me how your supervisor reacted?

Some interviewers might even smell blood at this point and become quite persistent. I have watched interviews fall apart during this query barrage. If you find yourself in this situation do not panic. Literally take a deep breath and slow down. You can change the pace of an interview by waiting several seconds to answer and talking slow.

A friend of mine uses this technique when we play poker. Every time one of the players gets on a lucky streak and wins several hands in a row, he slows the game down. He can stall better than anyone I have met. He will strike up a conversation, deal slowly, test everyone's patience by not being able to make a decision on a 'hit,' take a telephone call, develop memory loss, and even resort to drastic measures like spilling a drink. As childish as this all seems, his stalling works. The momentum is slowed and the luck of the table seems to change.

I am not suggesting you have memory loss or take a telephone call during an interview, *in fact I'm strongly recommending you do not.* The point is you can regroup and change the direction of an interview by altering the pace. The interviewer will lose interest when he or she realizes that you are not rattled. Your sudden seemingly methodical responses will throw the interviewer off their game.

One of my colleagues uses one different word when asking past behavioral questions. "**Will** you tell me about a time when you had to choose between honesty and dishonesty and how you made your decision?" This one word backs some candidates into a corner. Using the word 'will' to start the question indicates that the interviewer is sure that this has occurred, and that anything less than an admission might seem like insubordination.

Past behavioral questions are not always limited to work experience. Questions regarding school, personal, volunteer, or membership experiences might also be asked.

Future Situation or Hypothetical Questions

The purpose of future situation questions is to assess how the candidate might act under a specific set of circumstances. An example of a future situation question is:

Let's say that we have an exceptional employee with seniority that is out-producing all others by over one hundred per cent. This employee is punctual, never misses work, and is in all ways perfect except that he continually questions your decisions in front of other employees. He also happens to be a good friend of your supervisor. What would you do? Please limit your answer to three sentences.

Knowledge and Experience Questions

These are questions about your knowledge and experience.

Employer Secret 62: When a candidate is called for an interview, his or her knowledge and experience are not the biggest issues.

When you have been called for an interview, you have been called *because* of your knowledge and experience.

Few employees are fired because they lacked the knowledge and experience to do the job. Your knowledge and experience that are pertinent to the employer's opening are important, and your skill level might be tested. But finding out what kind of person you are, how you will behave, and how effectively you can apply your experience and knowledge are the employer's main concerns.

Verifying that you have the knowledge and experience you claim *is* an issue.

Verifiable Questions and Verified Questions

Verifiable questions are questions that the employer can verify. Verified questions are *verifiable* questions that the interviewer has *already verified.* These are not rhetorical questions because the interviewer expects an answer, and the fact that the interviewer knows the answer is not so obvious.

Employer Secret 52: Employers ask candidates questions about the candidates or their past that the employer already has the answer to.

Sometimes employers have already verified your past employment or done some investigative work before the interview.

If all of this is beginning to sound like a lot of hard work, you need to know that being prepared for a successful job interview is hard work – but I have good news.

Knocking Down Their House of Cards

Here's good news about interview questions:

- You already have the answers to past behavioral questions!
- Situational or hypothetical questions are not verifiable!
- You already have the answers to knowledge and experience questions!
- When it comes to the product which is '*you,*' you are the expert.
- Most employers will be asking other candidates for the same position basically the same questions.

Employer Secret 69: *During the job interview,* a rehearsed candidate with job selling skills has an advantage.

How can this be? After all the cards are stacked against the candidate. True. But the employer is *buying.* The employer is in the position of Company YOU.

If people really had to buy and pay for computers like Company YOU, they would be cautious and maybe even *paranoid.* As the computer salesperson (job candidate), you have almost all of the knowledge about the product the employer is considering. You are the expert on you and now you are learning the employers' secrets.

Know your resume,
practice job selling skills,
and remember, you are there to listen and learn
about the employer and their needs.

How do you turn an interview into a sales presentation?

Asking questions puts you in control and timing is critical.

Remember Listening Science Lesson Nine? Timing is critical. Again, do not walk in to an interview firing a barrage of questions. I always respond to the first three to five questions with one to three sentence answers, or yes or no. Then I start adding a question after my answer. I have been to or observed plenty of interviews where the interviewer does *not* give the candidate the opportunity to ask questions at the end of the interview. Again, I don't wait for an invitation to ask questions, and I don't care how tough their questions are, I still work mine in.

Tough Interview Questions and *My Answers*

- Why do you want to work for this company?

The answer to this question depends on the timing. If the question is being asked prematurely, before I have had the opportunity to ask questions about the company here is my answer: *I am not yet convinced that I do. Will you tell what you find most appealing about working here?*

If the question is asked late in the interview and after I have had the chance to ask what I wanted, here is my answer:
I find the company and position you have described exciting.
Will you tell what you find most appealing about working here?

- What makes you think you can do this job?

If this question is being asked prematurely, before the position has been discussed and before I have asked questions, here is my answer: *I do not have enough information about the position to tell you that I can do this job. Could you please tell me what you see in my qualifications and experience that make you believe I can do this job? (I am not looking for assurance here, I answer and ask with confidence in order to obtain information.)*

If the question is being asked after the position has been described I would answer: *I am confident that with my knowledge, experience, and enthusiasm, I can do this job. What makes you think I can do this job?*

- In what area do you feel you need improvement?

Since I consistently strive to improve myself in all areas at every opportunity, there is no specific listed skill in which I am not proficient. What are the specific challenges of this position that you think will require special attention?

- Are you punctual?

I have read that the first thirty minutes on the job are the most non productive as employees spend time becoming acclimated to their work environment. I have learned to arrive early to increase my productivity. Has tardiness been a management issue for you?

- Are you happy with your current employer?

I have a great deal of respect for my present employer. If I choose to leave I will give whatever notice my employer needs, within reason, to compensate for my position. If this period is as long as four weeks, will that be acceptable to you?

- What is your worst characteristic?

I sometimes expect the same level of company loyalty from others as my own. Are employees here happy with the company?

- Why are you leaving your present position?

If this question is asked before I have been offered the job, here is my answer: *I am not sure I will be leaving my current employer. That decision will be based on what information you provide me with about your company and my assessment of my ability to fulfill your needs. How soon will you be making a hiring decision?*

- What kind of people do you have a difficult time working with?

I enjoy most personality types but do not appreciate disloyal or dishonest people. What types of people do you consider difficult?

Remember Listening Science Lesson Four?
Ask Questions.

- Asking questions gets the other person talking and you listening.
- Asking questions puts you in control.
- Asking questions gets you information
- Asking questions helps you develop empathy.
- Asking questions develops trust.

Questions are the POWER of conversation. Most people like to talk and most people like to talk about themselves. Getting the other person to talk gets you information, helps you gain control of the conversation, and increases the time you will be listening and not talking. The more someone *talks to you* the more they *trust you.*

Design questions as a candidate to get the interviewer to sell to you. Interviewers are usually trained in selling the company. Anytime you can get the employer selling to you, you're in a stronger position.

◆──────────────◆

A silent pause illuminates conversation.

17. How You Can Survive These Interview Tricks

Employer Secret 62: Employers use the interrogation technique of silence.

Employers know that most job candidate's acts of past undesirable behavior or information inconsistencies are through voluntary admission and often occur *after* they have provided an answer during orchestrated moments of silence. The following is from an interview I conducted.

"So what exactly happened that caused you to leave your last job?" I asked.

"I was laid off," replied the candidate.

At this point I was not going to utter a single word until the candidate spoke again. The average time before the candidate will speak first is less than five seconds. Ten seconds of silence in an interview is a *very long time*.

"Well," the candidate continued, "there was a cut back in man power."

This was followed by less than five seconds of silence.

"I mean there had been several incidents of inventory theft and management decided to clean house," stated the candidate.

I simply peered over the resume I was holding and remained silent.

"It didn't matter how honest I was or even if I knew who was involved," they let five of us go.

"I think it was because my boss was jealous of me. I got away with so much more before he came."

Whether or not this candidate was guilty of anything or not the statements did not yield any level of confidence for me.

I can not tell you how many times this simple technique of silence has resulted in rambling by the candidate and even confessions of unacceptable behavior.

After answering a question, when faced with silence, either ask a question or remain silent.

Employer Secret 99: The more you can get them to say, the better the chance they will betray.

I have heard this saying regarding job candidates and interviews uttered discreetly among colleagues in more than one Human Resource department. This is one more reason to use the 'Nine Lessons of Listening Science.' The more you listen the less you say. Maybe the counter saying for job candidates should be "The less you say the longer you'll stay."

Employer Secret 51: Employers use the third party question.

The third party question is designed to get candidates to speak more openly about themselves. Examples:

How would your last boss describe you?

How would your coworkers describe you?

Employer Secret 53: Employers ask questions to throw you off your game plan. (Early salary questions for example)

Fishing Questions

Fishing questions are just that. The interrogator doesn't know the answer, and is just throwing his or her line in the water hoping you take the bait. Here are some examples of 'fishing questions;'

- So what is the real reason you left your last job?
- What kind of pay are you really looking for?
- In addition to that, what else happened?
- How much experience do you have for this position?
- What do you think your previous employers are saying about you?
  This question insinuates that the interviewer has spoken to your previous employers.
- If I offer you the job right now, would you take it? **(CAUTION: This is not a job offer.)**

Employer Secret 50: Employers will purposely plan interview interruptions.

I used to play tennis with a friend and he was fiercely competitive. We would usually play on an outdoor court in the afternoon during the summer, for an hour or so several times per week. I was always able to win every game of the first half we played. Then we would take a break and I would get a cold drink. My competitor would go to the locker room where I presumed he was using the restroom.

My friend would return and win the first several games after the break. Years later, I discovered he was retreating to the locker room where he would take a quick, cool shower. This would lower his body temperature and rejuvenate him while I waited in the heat outdoors.

I have known employers who have planned interruptions during an interview. Suddenly they must leave the room to take a call or attend to some other urgent matter. During this time some regroup and others watch the candidate through a two-way mirror. I know one employer who uses this time to review his notes on everything the candidate has stated. He then returns with questions designed to trip up the candidate.

The best you can do as a candidate during these periods is relax and wait. Do not snoop through the pile of resumes left as a lure of temptation on the desk in front of you. Never read anything left on the desk or tables around you.

Employer Secret 97: The 'gang interview' is often used to put candidates under pressure.

This type of interview can actually be beneficial. Your strategy and success in the 'gang interview' depends on your 'job selling' skills. Although many of the same 'job selling' skills apply, being interviewed by several people at once presents new dynamics. Usually 'gang interviews' are not done at the initial interview, but a second or third meeting. This is good because at this point you have impressed the original interviewer and you are still in the running.

The 'gang interview' could be a peer interview. These are the people you would be working with. Peer interviews can be very beneficial. They can be done in a gang setting or a series of one on one mini interviews, usually taking place in one day. These interviews can give you new insight by meeting the personalities you would be working with. If you know ahead of time the employer is going to be conducting peer interviews, you can design your questions accordingly. What do you want to know from these people? Information that will help you assess their needs and desires.

- *How do you like working here?*
- *If I take this position, what could I be doing that would help you?*
- *What challenges do you see for the position I am applying for?*

In either a gang or peer interview, remember what has not changed. You are there to:

Learn your customer's needs and desires.
Empathize with their position.
Assess if you *can and want* to meet their needs and desires.
and later step four...

Persuade your customer that you can *help them* meet those needs and desires better than anyone else on the planet.

Remember, in order for you to be able to assess if you *can and want* to meet the employer's needs and desires, you will need information about the position pertinent to *your expectations*. Although you need to focus on the customer's needs and desires, do not neglect your own. Satisfying your needs and desires is an element that is paramount to your employer's best interests. Interviews with potential peers is a great opportunity to gather information pertinent to assessing the position to determine if you *want* to meet the employer's needs and desires.

Many employers will have briefed employees on interview conduct previous to peer meetings. Some employees will be reluctant to answer some questions. Here are key questions you should try to work in to peer interviews.

- *How long have you been with the company?*
- *What opportunities do you have for advancement?*
- *How often does the company have performance evaluations?*
- *This is just a yes or no question- Have you ever had any negative or positive surprises during a performance evaluation?* You might not get an answer to this question but if you do the information is invaluable to you. No one should be surprised in a performance evaluation. These types

of surprises would indicate poor management communication in daily activity.

- *Do you have all the authority you need to do your job?*
- *How many bosses or supervisors do you have?*
- *Could you describe the work atmosphere?*

You should not need to concentrate on persuading every person you meet in a peer interview or gang setting but you should always be practicing 'job selling skills.' If peer interviews are done in a series of one on one interviews, treat each one with the same importance as your initial company interview. You will have no way of knowing how much influence any of these people will have in a final decision.

Remember to fly your flag at each one. Practice the first three steps of LEAP in these settings and save persuading to your last meeting or follow up meeting with the key person you will be dealing with. After meeting with all of these different people you need a little time to digest the information and assess if you *can and want* to meet their needs and desires.

*There is one irresistible act
that will make other people like you.*

18. The Simple Act That Makes Employers Like You

In grade school there was a teacher everyone dreaded, Ms. Scrugg. She had a reputation that made even teenagers shudder. Kids said she hated everyone. She had been in an accident that had left part of her face paralyzed so she looked as though she was always scorning. The mere sight of her in the hallway made us take the long way around. Rumor was that she had never given anyone a grade higher than a C.

I will never forget when my fall class schedule arrived one late summer day. As I scanned the itinerary one name stood out on that card as if it had been typed in bold face in a font five times the size of anything else on the page:

Ms. Scrugg

That letter dimmed my enjoyment of the last two weeks of summer vacation.

When school started I reported to Ms. Scrugg's class late and the only chair left was a desk in the front that faced hers. In fact the front of my desk was resting against the front of her desk. She announced that these seats would be our permanent places for the semester. I would be face to face with her everyday. I was mortified.

I found her quite unattractive, her speech was impaired, and she had steely eyes. She seemed very cold and did not show any hint of emotion. Her teaching was robotic and she answered questions in as few syllables as possible. Even so, once in a while I would catch her stepping out of character.

Maybe because I sat so close to her I noticed that when other classes were outside playing, she would gaze out the window with a slight smile. Once I broke a shoelace and she bent down and temporarily repaired the cord with some string.

Over the next few weeks I noticed that during the times the class was working, Ms. Scrugg would open the drawer to her desk and retrieve a prescription bottle. She would cup her hand around the bottle as if to keep anyone from seeing, but from my position I saw it. She would often swallow more than one pill during the one-hour class period.

She had told us she had no children, but revealed little else about herself. I noticed that she kept a small, framed picture of a young boy on her desk.

One day I stayed after class to ask a question, regarding an assignment. We were alone in the room when my curiosity got the best of me. "Ms. Scrugg," I questioned, who is the boy in the picture on the corner of your desk?"

"That was my son," she responded. "I lost him in an auto accident."

"Oh," I replied.

"Yes that was seven years ago."

"Is that the same accident that hurt you?" I queried.

After a pause she answered, "Yes"

"And you are still in pain?"

She looked surprised. "What makes you think I'm in pain?"

"Because you take pills."

"Yes sometimes I am... in pain."

I retorted with what seemed like the most logical question at the time. "Then why do you work?" After all, my Dad didn't go to work when he was in pain. She turned and looked out the window.

"The pills are for the pain in my face and body. My work is for the pain in my heart."

The answer was much more profound than I was prepared to respond to at ten years of age, so I left for home.

I wrote a poem later expressing how she would serve her son's memory better by breaking down her walls and becoming closer to the children now in her care.

Without the hesitation of maturity, I gave her the poem. She never mentioned the poem, still the next day she cried when she spoke to me.

Ms. Scrugg called on me often after that and smiled when she saw me. The other students noticed but they did not call me the 'teacher's pet.' Any change in her demeanor was so welcome that no matter what the reason none of them wanted to risk any regression. She taught us the importance of each day and the meaning of taking people for granted.

Ms. Scrugg was not a bad teacher, just sad. She was kind and had never spoken an ill word about anyone in the classroom.

I didn't really understand exactly why she liked me until years later. The simplistic answer is this: One irresistible act will make other people like you.

Like them first.

Typical interviews are employers asking the same set of questions to each candidate and deciding which candidate they *liked* the most. Yes I said liked. People buy from people they *like*. Employers hire qualified candidates they *like*. You will greatly increase your chances of success by being likable. Find something in the other person you like.

When is the last time you made a major purchase from someone that you did not like? If you *like* the computer salesperson coming to see you at Company YOU, doesn't that make trusting him or her easier? People generally do not trust people they do not like.

Become *likeable* by being *able to like*.

Section IV Summary

Employer Secret 65: Interviewers eliminate more than one half of candidates in the first five minutes.

The majority of hiring decisions are influenced in the first five minutes of a job interview, these five minutes become the most important five minutes of your career. Fly your flag!

There are several general question category types used by employers that can be classified as follows:

- Past behavioral questions
- Future situation questions
- Knowledge and Experience questions
- Verified Questions
- Verifiable Questions

You already have the answers to past behavioral questions!
Situational or hypothetical questions are not verifiable!
You already have the answers to knowledge and
experience questions!

There is one irresistible act
that will make other people like you.
Like them first.
Become *likeable* by being *able to like.*

For more information on interview questions and tactics
visit
www.employersecrets.com

▼▼▼▼▼▼▼▼▼▼▼▼▼▼▼▼▼▼▼▼▼▼▼▼▼▼▼▼▼▼▼▼▼▼▼▼

V. Employer Secrets and Negotiation

Often your most valued possession – your opinion,
is your least appreciated gift.
The offering of your viewpoint will be more accepted
when wrapped in consideration.

19. Why the Old Laws of Negotiation Are Not Working

Two primitive men once met at cliffs, each on the opposite side of a deep impassable ravine. As they surveyed their options they simultaneously saw a vine growing across the wide crevice between two trees. Each man grabbed one end of the vine and began to pull. What resulted was a tug of war. Both men had a similar objective, to cross the ravine, yet each man was convinced that if he possessed the vine he would achieve his goal. Finally one man won out and succeeded in dropping his opponent into the ravine. As the man fell he clung to the vine and the other man was forced to let go or meet with the same fate. Now one man lay at the bottom of the ravine with the vine and the other stood at the top with no way to the other side.

Many negotiations are much like this tug of war. Sometimes both sides lose and in the best case only one side wins.

Most negotiation is about trying to get what you want by sacrificing as little as possible of what you have. Little thought is given to the other party and when time is spent thinking about them, the interest is from your perspective and what you want. This creates a constant battle that is doomed to failure, or at best, difficult negotiation and improbable results.

<u>What should negotiation be?</u>

Trying to understand *exactly* what the other party *really* wants and why and finding out how to fulfill this need in exchange for what you want. The focus is on the other party's needs. If you understand them *from their point of view* and fulfill those exact needs from their perspective you will most often get what you want.

Most of us are familiar with the old standard sayings or laws of negotiation. **These old sayings do not all work for job negotiation. Job negotiation is different.**

<u>What's different about job negotiation?</u>

In the following comparisons, I have used the transaction of property because other than a job, a home is the largest and closest size comparable negotiation that an average person will make in his or her lifetime, and because most all the old laws of negotiation were designed generally for buy/sell situations.

1.   When you negotiate the sale of a house, when the house is sold, you usually don't deal with the buyers again.

When you negotiate for a job, after the negotiation is over, you will deal with the employer for forty hours per week and depend on them for your income, maybe for years.

2.   The average participant is on fairly equal negotiation ground with the other party (buyer or seller) of a home.
*When you sell or buy a home you are usually dealing with a **person.***
*When you are job negotiating you are usually dealing with **personnel** (they are being paid.)*
Employers are people too, but the point is negotiating with them is different than dealing with individuals.
Employers, including small business owners and human resource personnel, often have extensive negotiation experience. They know the old laws and practice them.

3.   Homebuyers and sellers are commonly represented by real estate agents.
Most job candidates are not represented by agents.

4.   In a property transaction, the act of negotiating generally has one general purpose for each party – the buyer wants to buy and the seller wants to sell.
Depending on the type of position, employers might have ulterior motives, such as quotas.

Employer Secret 74: The negotiation process in and of itself is often a test for the candidate and sometimes for the negotiator (employer.)

5.   When you buy a house, the asking price is always
     known.
     *An abundance of employers advertise no pay
     whatsoever. Applying for a job when the salary is
     not known can be advantageous to the employer.*

6.   In a property transaction, the seller and buyer are
     usually negotiating for their own money.
     *Unless the business is privately held and you are
     negotiating with an owner, the personnel or
     employees are often not negotiating with their own
     money. The majority of employers are employees
     negotiating with company money.*

7.   Most of the time, a home buyer already has a roof
     over head.
     Most job hunters are out of work or soon will be.

◆————————————◆

20. The Seven New Laws of Job Negotiation

New Law One

Old Negotiation Law: Everything is negotiable.
New Negotiation Law 1: *Your performance is not negotiable.*

I received a call from a rather large firm that had been referred to me for consulting services. When I reached their office I was introduced to the company president, Mr. Holmes. I had heard Mr. Holmes was used to getting his way and he was a boisterous mountain of a man at six foot seven inches. I am sure many people struggled just to reckon with his presence.

"Hello, Mr. Baker. I've heard good things about you," he bellowed as his handshake swallowed my hand.

After a lengthy discussion of his needs and my solutions, he asked my fee. This was a complex job that would require numerous hours still I quoted the normal fee.

"My fee is three hundred dollars per hour."

"I will pay you one hundred fifty," he flatly stated.

"I'm not sure you'd like that Mr. Holmes," I replied.

"And why is that?" he puzzled.

"Because that will limit me to making only a fifty per cent effort."

"What?" he said resoundingly.

"I learned long ago that compromising pay diminishes performance."

"Surly two hundred fifty an hour is reasonable," he stated.

"If I reduced my fee, I believe that you are so business savvy you would not want to hire me."

"Why's that?" he asked.

"Because that would mean I just quoted you a fee that was above my value. Based on my expert knowledge in my field, my record of results, and your project, I know my value. I stated my value to you in complete honesty and fairness. If I reduced my fee now, would you think that perhaps I was not knowledgeable enough to have known my own value? Therefore wouldn't I possibly be an inferior candidate for the job?"

"Well I know most of you consultants come in here expecting to chaffer for your fees," he stated.

"Then obviously I am not like the run of the mill consultant. I did not quote you an inflated fee on the off chance that you were going to offer me less and if you did not, collect more from you than my work is worth."

"Mr. Baker, I pride myself in my negotiation skills, yet it seems that in less than two minutes you have stopped me dead in my tracks. How soon can you get started?"

This one job bred more work from recommendations by Mr. Holmes. That first encounter reinforced what I have learned from selling and negotiating. Reducing price, diminishes the value. Stick by your guns!

Imagine this job negotiation:
Employer: "The top of our salary range is considerably more than we have offered you. But we feel our lower offer best fits your past experience."
Candidate: "As you know, your offer is twenty per cent less than my previous salary. I am willing to accept this offer for my performance of twenty per cent less effort on the job."

Employers are not buying your past experience, they are buying your future performance. They are simply trying to predict your future performance based on their limited information of your past.

Keep this in mind when negotiating. You are the product. But the employer is buying your future performance.

For example, when you buy a used car you do not pay for the past performance or previous owner's use of the car. If you are a prudent shopper, you might ask questions about the history of the vehicle and inspect the present condition. But you are buying the use of the future performance of that vehicle.

The employer is using the past as a negotiating tool in his favor. The candidate is responding logically.

I once had ten Hank Aaron baseball cards for sale, all identical. I knew each was worth $ 5.00 so I wanted exactly $ 50.00 for all ten. A fellow offered me forty dollars for the set. I told him he could have eight cards for $ 40.00 I knew the cards were worth $ 5.00 each and would be easy to sell.

In a job negotiation, *when you know your value*, and you know the market will bear it, why would you take less? Once you have a job, you usually cannot or at least should not hold back some of your dedication or performance based on your pay. Your time is usually committed and you couldn't sell any remaining portion of performance even if you wanted to. Selling your dedication and performance is an *all or nothing* deal.

The exceptions to this might be a performance based pay contract such as in sports or a commission job. (A commission job will usually pay everyone the same commission per sale unless based upon a certain volume achieved in a period of time.)

New Law Two

Old Negotiation Law: Whoever mentions a number first loses.

New Negotiation Law 2: Whoever mentions a number first *chooses.*

If the old law were correct, that would mean in every negotiation there are a winner and a loser. This flies in the face of all win/win philosophy.

What happens when both parties follow this old law? You have a deadlock before any negotiations have started.

It's what number you mention and how that counts!

If you get the number you want you win.

Employers are used to working within a pay range of numbers. In job negotiations, the employer has almost always established a salary range for every position. Often this salary or pay range is posted with the job announcement. At this point, you have the opportunity to choose to accept or reject the range. An employer established salary range is a scale that *only measures the candidate's ability to sell and negotiate.*

Employer Secret 76: In most cases, a salary range is a scale that only measures *your ability to negotiate.*

When an employer refuses to reveal a number, backs you into a corner by asking what pay you want, and negotiations stall, you risk the employer terminating negotiations because they often have the upper hand. When you are going to state a number, do the homework and give the employer a salary range. *Make sure your high number is the bottom of the range, and if they accept your range for negotiating, you can't lose.*

For example: If you know you want a $120,000. salary, the range you state should be $120,000. to $150,000.

You are the product. You know yourself better than anyone else. When you go to a job interview that is the sales presentation. Your job is to learn the employer's need and determine whether your qualifications can fill it. Do you know yourself well enough? Few people assess themselves correctly. Why? They are not qualified, they are biased, and how they see themselves is often not how others see them. Do banks ask you to appraise your own house? No, because even if you were qualified you would be biased. You have to know what you are worth. How can you get an accurate evaluation of yourself?

In order to negotiate a salary or pay, you must know your value. Do you know how to value yourself? What is your life worth? Not what is your net worth, *what is your life worth?* Do you know what your education and experience is worth? What about dedication, loyalty, honesty, and dependability?

Throughout this book I've talked about focusing on the interests of your employer first. Because your interests are second *does not mean they are worth any less.* In fact, *you will be worth more.* You will be worth more because most candidates and employees do not focus on the employer's interests and therefore are generally less desirable and less productive. You will be worth more because your focus will demonstrate value to the employer. If you can truly practice putting the interests of your employer first, you will always be worth more than the average employee.

Putting your employer's interests first, never means you need become a doormat, or kiss up. *Keeping yourself happy is a part of putting your employer's interests first.*

We've heard that everything is worth what someone will pay for it. Most people believe they are worth either their 'net worth' or their annual income. I remember in grade school a teacher told our class a human being was made up of chemicals worth $1.98. (There have been times in my life when my net worth was no more the value of my chemical make up.)

If something is worth what someone will pay for it does this mean that the same product or service could have a different value to different people? YES. Often people will buy the same item for very different prices.

Worth is based on perception of value.

A mediocre marketing manager with five years experience might start a new position at $ 100,000. annual salary, while a new graduate with exceptional qualities is paid $75,000.

Experience creates a perception of value. Selling skills create value. The possibility of unavailability creates a perception of value.

Desperation, unlimited accessibility, abundance, and a lack of value building skills all **diminish** value.

Selling skills often overcome many qualification deficits.

<u>Worth is based on perception of need or desire.</u>

A store that has just lost their marketing manager might be so desperate as to offer a much higher than normal starting salary. Perception of need dictates value.

<u>Worth is based on supply and demand.</u>

Marketing managers on the east coast might be abundant and therefore are paid a starting salary of $50,000 annually, while in short supply on the west coast they are paid a starting salary of $ 85,000.

<u>You can use selling skills to increase the perception of value.</u>

Two marketing managers of equal experience, knowledge, skills, and ability might have quite different salaries based on only one difference. One may be able to create a more valuable perception.

The more value a customer perceives, the more a customer will pay. In fact, the best selling is about value and not about price. The best job selling is about value and not about salary.

Employer Secret 116: A good employer won't like you at a bargain price.

Why? People perceive that things are worth what they are paying for them. Anytime an employer knows that competitors are paying considerably more for employees with experience and skills similar to yours, the employer will believe either that you are not as good as competitors' employees or that you have some hidden defect, otherwise you would leave.

If you know that you are worth considerably more than you are being paid or more than the earning potential of a position, you will eventually become unhappy and your performance will suffer.

New Law Three

Old Negotiation Law: The strongest negotiation tool is the ability to walk away from the table.

New Negotiation Law 3:   Before you walk away from their table, *make sure you have food on your table.*

When I was younger and quite naïve I took on the local utility company. I was moving into a new apartment and requested the electricity be changed to my name on the first of the next month. The power company mistakenly put the power in my name that day. When I moved in I received a bill for the previous month, while the other tenants had occupied the apartment. This happened during a hot summer so when I moved into my new place I received a sizable bill.

After several weeks of unsuccessful conversations with the power company, they threatened to disconnect my electricity unless I paid. I was getting nowhere and remember saying something like "I dare you," and 'walking away' from the negotiation table by hanging up the phone.

That night I returned home late. Sitting alone in the dark apartment I said, "I really showed them." My food was already rotting in the refrigerator. Of course I had to do without television, radio, and my computer. After only a few minutes I decided to pay the bill, but my cell phone battery was dead and needed charging.

The moral of the story is:

Don't try to negotiate… *without power!*

Why does it seem when you get one job offer you often get another? Confidence. When you have more than one offer you have power.

Why do you seem to always get the offer when you really don't want the job? Confidence. When you really don't want the job, you are more confident or you exuberate an indifference that is easily interpreted as confidence.

If out of work, you should strive for simultaneous offers from several employers. Because, commonly, the only way most people can afford to walk away from the job negotiation table, is if they have another job or offer. If you have a job, try to stay employed until you land another one. Having another job or offer gives you the power to walk away.

Another way to increase your position of power is to maintain your state of learning throughout negotiations.

When you go to an interview for the purpose of learning, you have nothing at stake. Seeing the whole process as the opportunity to learn more about the employer and sharpen your negotiation skills, gives you great power.

Always operate from a position of strength.

You can't always be in a position of strength,

but you can always *operate* from a position of strength.

New Law Four

Old Negotiation Law: Look out for number one.
New Negotiation Law 4: If you consider yourself number one, *look out.*

If a salesperson arrived at Company YOU, and showed little concern for your interests by trying to get you to buy before she even demonstrated the computer or without allowing you to ask questions, she probably would not have much of a chance with you or her next customer. Salespeople quit sales jobs and even more lose sales everyday because their customers just aren't buying. So many salespeople tell me they quit a job because the product or service they were selling just wasn't any good.

Either they did not have the selling skills needed and were focusing on themselves or they did not evaluate the job well during the hiring process. If the reason they were not selling was because the product or service really wasn't any good, then they did not evaluate the job well during the hiring process, and instead of admitting that, they are protecting their ego. Too much ego can prevent sales, cause havoc, and even inflict harm to one's self.

A business associate of mine, Mr. Goldstein, often invited me to lunch to hear the latest merger and acquisition scuttlebutt. He was a good friend, and now and then I teased him about his enormous ego. What I hadn't known was how enormous his ego really was.

One day over our usual gourmet burgers (the restaurant put 'Grey Poupon' on a cheeseburger), I told Mr. Goldstein about a company I had considered purchasing. The business was not much more than a start up at only twenty-four months old and almost at the breakeven point.

The industry was booming and this company had a government contract worth millions. There was a dispute between the two partners and the one with the money was leaving. The departing owner, the majority stockholder, wanted only his original investment returned which was a nominal sum. The deal appeared to be a steal.

Mr. Goldstein listened intently. When I discussed the numbers I watched his eyes grow as big as silver dollars. Before lunch was over he insisted on meeting with the two partners.

The next week we sat down with the partner that wanted to stick with the business, Tim. He was quite knowledgeable and down to earth. Even though his expertise was far beyond Mr. Goldstein's and mine, Tim explained his business in easy to understand terms. The potential for the company was extraordinary. Besides the government contract, there were several new international accounts. Tim did mention there was a critical supplier that was having trouble delivering.

As we left the meeting, Mr. Goldstein was so ready to buy out the other partner he asked me to draw up the papers as soon as I returned to the office. I cautioned him that we had not yet met the other partner. He said "I don't need to. He won't be around anyway."

When I reminded him about the supplier issue his response was, "If they can't do the job we'll find another supplier. I am the customer."

Mr. Goldstein spoke like he already owned the company. *When someone starts talking and placing himself in the future tense, keeping him (or her) from going there can be impossible.* I cautioned him to perform more due diligence several times, yet he was like an unstoppable train.

"I know the opportunity of a lifetime when I see it," he said.

Now I say once in a lifetime opportunities come along everyday, even so, I always investigate. After several more meetings the deal went smoothly and Mr. Goldstein closed on the business in just three weeks.

As Mr. Goldstein was very busy our lunches were less frequent. Each time I did see him he bragged, in front of our colleagues and me, about what an excellent investment he had made and how he had 'stole' the business.

Just four weeks later I got the first of several heartbreaking calls from Mr. Goldstein's new partner, Tim. Seems that critical supplier was now a critical issue. The supplier manufactured a part that was necessary for Mr. Goldstein's final product. The part was specified in the government contract and the supplier held a patent on the part. The issue was the supplier had agreed only to sell ten thousand units to Mr. Goldstein's company and those had been purchased. The supplier knew how lucrative the government contract was and now wanted in on the deal. The supplier offered Mr. Goldstein a deal he couldn't refuse. Either he could pay them their price, or they would compete with him.

This was just the beginning of the nightmare for Mr. Goldstein. After only six months the business had cost him over five times his initial investment. He stopped asking me to lunch altogether and when I saw him at a social gathering he conveniently slipped away.

Mr. Goldstein had a network of friends that were all experts in business. Yet he avoided all of them including me to avoid admitting that he had made a mistake. He continued to throw good money after bad in an effort to revive the company and maintain his ego. His ego was way overpriced.

An ego is not a necessarily a bad thing. A man or woman with no ego would have low self-esteem. But an ego that stands in the way of good business sense or causes harm to others or one's self *is bad*.

Practicing the four steps of LEAP has always focused my selling on the other party.

New Law Five

Old Negotiation Law: Don't leave money on the table.
New Negotiation Law 5: Don't put your money on the table.

This old law usually refers to paying too much or charging too little for something. In the case of job negotiating, make sure you know exactly what the job is because that's what you are charging for. Your performance and time are your products. In most job situations, you are selling your time, *because that's how they are paying you.* Exceptions to this are commission-based jobs and profit percentage based bonus plans. In those cases you are being paid for performance.

The ways you 'undercharge' for the service you are providing an employer are:

1) Negotiating and accepting an unsuitable salary
2) Committing to extraordinary hours
3) Accepting a position that does not define hours

You can certainly undercharge for a job by the amount of responsibility handed you or by working in a stressful environment. During the hiring and negotiating process you are responsible for assessing the duties and job description. What are the two biggest employee complaints within one year on the job? (from Chapter 3)

> 1. "The job is not what I expected."
> 2. "I am not making enough money."

Don't commit to a job or accept an offer until you know what the employer expects of you. The job description the employer has advertised or provides you might be snake oil.

Don't put your money on the table by committing to a salary before you know the job. Ask questions.

Don't commit, until you know the job will fit.

New Law Six

Old Negotiation Law: Drive a hard bargain.

New Negotiation Law 6: Don't be hard to bargain with.

Mr. Harvey selected me as the chosen candidate for a contract position for one of his companies. We had reached the negotiation stage and I knew this would be a long-term contract that could also lead to referrals for more work.

He presented a salary that was fair at ten per cent less than what I had requested. After I rejected the offer, he requested a meeting with me. After some brief chit chat the conversation got down to business.

"Mr. Baker, why did you reject my offer?" he inquired.

"Because I am sure you wouldn't want to pay a penny less. I'm just guessing but your salary offer is probably the same as or less than the last person you had in this position. With the information you have given me about the present condition of the business and the moral of the employees, I know I will be performing at a higher level than your last manager. I am certain you don't expect anything less." (Just so happens I found out later I was right 'on the money.')

"Well I certainly appreciate that but I'm just not sure we can afford you," he responded.

"I don't want you to sell this company short. You have told me that getting a new manager in place as soon as possible is critical. Isn't that correct?"

"Yes," he responded.

"When I quoted you my salary requirement, I gave you my best offer to save you the time of bantering. My skills are going to increase your profits within days of my employment. Everyday we waste in negotiating will cost you money. The risk of waiting might cost you far more than the small variance we are now discussing."

"That is true," Mr. Harvey pondered.

"As you are an expert at making decisions, I am here because you now know I'm the best person for this job. Do you really want to spend more time looking, then settling for less, even for a possible small variance in price?"

"Of course I don't," Mr. Harvey replied.

"I don't want you to have to either. I am looking forward to starting right away. Shall we work together?" Mr. Harvey paid my price.

During negotiating, I have learned to start every response in the customer's interest and *always say everything with a smile.* When you negotiate for a job after the deal is over you will 'deal' with the employer for forty hours per week and depend on them for your income, maybe for years.

New Law Seven

Old Negotiation Law : Never let them see you sweat.
New Negotiation Law 7: Let them know that once you are hired, you will work up a sweat.

As in the seven laws of persuasion you must *assure* the employer of what they are buying. Remember employers are buying future performance and you are selling future performance. Don't settle for the pay you were getting on your last job. Salary history should remain just that, history.

Make sure the employer knows you are going to give them
a stellar performance.
Make sure they are *persuaded.*

EARN the job offer.

Ten Ways to Build Your Value

1. Talk in terms of the employer's interests even during negotiations.
2. Remind the employer of why they called you in the first place – because your skills and experience are what they are looking for. *Each time* they talk a lower figure than the one you want, start discussing your experience, skills, and assessment of their challenges and your solutions.
3. Consistently remind them of their needs and desires.
4. Be a limited edition. In other terms, make sure they know you are available only for a short time.
5. Let them know you are considering other offers.
6. If you are employed, subtly remind them.
7. Do not jump at their offer. Always sleep on it.
8. Use the 'Seven A's of Persuasion' during negotiation. Operate from a position of strength. (A strong negotiator builds value just by demonstrating good negotiating skills.)
9. Be firm but remain likeable. Likeability builds value.
10. Let them know your performance is not negotiable and you know the value.

◆———————————◆

Top pay can be found on the bottom line.

21. This One Secret Can Get You Top Pay

Business is about profit. *It makes no difference how much people are paid if they produce acceptably more profit than their expense (and they can prove it.)*

Employer Secret 77: Almost all employers can pay more than they tell you for almost all jobs.

Employer Secret 78: Many employers will allow you to negotiate a future raise when you are hired.
(If they will not pay you the top of the pay range, try bargaining for higher pay effective at a future date.)

Most positions either directly or indirectly contribute to profit. Every job is contributing to either the expense or revenue side of the accounting equation. After years of consulting, I have discovered that most companies have no idea where the 'break even' salary is on any of their employees. Therefore most employers and employees have no idea whether employees are actually contributing to their company's bottom line or not. Despite that every employee should be instructed on how their job affects profit and be empowered to produce profit, this is not the case.

Most employers have a salary range or pay range in mind when they set out to hire. Where do they come up with these figures? While some base these figures on internal data still most are strictly based on competitive salaries from surveys, other sources, and you.

Have you ever seen this in a 'help wanted' ad?
Include salary requirements
or
Include salary history

Employer Secret 1: Sometimes there is no job. Some employers place or post job openings just to gather salary data.

In fact, I once met a consultant who produced a survey by placing dummy help wanted ads in papers and on the Internet requesting salary information. He sold the data collection to businesses and HR departments.

Employers want to know your salary history. Can you blame them? Remember when you were shopping for a computer at Company YOU? The brochures you were receiving did not come with any pricing.

Some employers collect pay information just to read the market for certain industries or positions. Employers gather this information for several reasons. Employers read the market to find out the minimum amount they can get away with paying an employee. Employers want to find out if they are paying their present employees appropriately. After all, if their present employees are already at or above the market rate of pay, they can predict the odds of losing some employees when denying raises or handing down pay cuts. Sometimes employers need to budget for a particular position or want to find out what it will take to hire away a competitor's employees.

Pay is most often based on what other companies are paying for such a position, your salary history, or a combination of both. Then employers play the negotiation game.

Due to privacy laws and policies, Human Resource departments do not disclose present or past employees' salaries. Yet these same HR departments ask job applicants for their salary history. In this case, I say HR stands for 'Hypocritical Researchers.'

This is one of the best job candidate responses I've had (when I was an employer playing a hypocritical researcher) to my question; "What is your salary history?"

"My last employer gave me a pay raise of five percent after only one year of service. Without any official evaluation, I was surprised to receive a performance bonus of ten per cent of my annual salary the second year. In year three I was awarded another five per cent pay raise and last year I helped the company reach the highest level of annual sales ever."

Without revealing a single number this candidate answered the question and shined like a star. (This answer could have backfired though if she had just been laid off because the company was cutting back. Then I would not necessarily have attributed her salary climb to performance but suspected poor upper management.)

It would be nice if employers had a job description that included a 'profit range.' Job candidates would know what they could expect to earn based on their skills and effort and not the sole judgment of a boss or manager or on the basis of some measure of activity. Most often this is not the case. If so the objective would be:

To assess the job you need done and determine whether or not my skills and experience will produce optimum position profitability for you.

'Position Profitability' Now there's a new catch phrase, sometimes confused with ROI, (Return On Investment.) It's one thing to use familiar key words and catch phrases, and quite another to use a new one. When you use unique terms your vocabulary becomes refreshing and intriguing. (A word of caution: Do not overuse unique terms or use terms that no one can understand. There is always a fine line between intriguing and annoying by appearing arrogant.)

For years, employers have measured job performance by activity instead of productivity or position profitability. The employer has equated multi-tasking, extra duties, overtime, and the appearance of being busy, to productivity.

Learn the worth of the position to the company. This is often overlooked. Many job candidates have shorted themselves at the bargaining table by not knowing the worth of the position.

If you are going to be in a position to produce a sizable profit for a company, why should you take the job for only a poultry per-cent of that potential?

Position profitability is not to be confused with *'position probability.'*

I once did a 'position profitability' study for an employer (privately held company) with five people with the same job descriptions. Their salaries had been based on seniority, attendance, promptness, and attitude.

The basic break down was this:

	Annual Pay	Time On Job	Attendance	Attitude
Employee One	$60,000	2 Years	Good	Average
Employee Two	$52,000	3 Years	Good	Average
Employee Three	$75,000	3 Years	Average	Average
Employee Four	$68,000	4 Years	Perfect	Poor
Employee Five	$80,000	5 Years	Average	Average

After a 'position profitability' study their ratings were
(The higher the rating the more profit being produced.)

PP Rating

Employee One	1120
Employee Two	1230
Employee Three	780
Employee Four	170
Employee Five	190

Let's compare these ratings with the previous data:

	PP Rating	Annual Pay	Time On Job
Employee One	1120	$60,000	2 Years
Employee Two	1230	$52,000	3 Years
Employee Three	780	$75,000	3 Years
Employee Four	170	$68,000	4 Years
Employee Five	190	$80,000	5 Years

The higher the PP rating is, the more profitable the employee. *What all this data tells us is that the longer employees worked here the worse their actual value to the company became!*

As you can see there is no correlation between the amount of profit being generated for the employer and the employee's rate of pay. All the employees had to do to continue getting raises was to keep showing up. With continually more time on their hands, employees four and five with the most seniority were figuring out exactly how little they could do and keep their jobs. (Last I knew they were still employed at this same company and their PP ratings were continuing to drop so the employer is either ignoring my findings or hasn't figured out what to do!)

The average break-even point for this job was a score of 290. (Including revenue and indirect support formulas in the first year with a starting pay of $50,000.)   So the two most senior employees are actually losing money for the company.

The PP Rating is a number derived at based on a scale after consideration of the data.

So how can you use this type of information when negotiating a salary with a prospective employer?

First, ask the employer if there has been a 'position profitability' study performed for the job you are negotiating for.   If not, you could recommend they have one done by a competent consultant. (Do not attempt this yourself. This often requires an abundance of experience and confidential information that companies are not going to divulge to any job applicant.)

If the interviewer has no such study or does not know what you are referring to, ask if they know how the position affects company profit. Do they have any dollar amounts associated with profit and the position you are applying for?

If you still do not get an adequate answer, ask the employer what the *job expectations* are *(not the job description.)*

In our analogy of Company YOU, the job description would be what the computer will be doing for you each day. The job expectations would be how fast you expect the computer to perform, how long you expect the computer to last, how much downtime you expect to have, and what additional equipment you expect the computer to be compatible with.

Ask the employer how those expectations equate to the profit and loss statement (the bottom line) of the company.

Ask the employer how these expectations could be exceeded and how that might affect profits.

Remember that you are only trying to determine the employer's exact needs for your skills and experience and the cost to help you negotiate better. Some human resource personnel might be put off or intimidated by these types of questions. Many people conducting interviews do not have the information you are asking for or have the authority to make these kinds of decisions. I know you will be getting attention for asking these types of questions, just remember, not all strategies will work in all situations. Remain professional and friendly.

One job hunter that came to me for advice was turned down for five positions in six months before he found an employer who was intrigued by his line of questioning. He negotiated by selling value and received a starting pay of twenty five per cent more than advertised and a profit sharing agreement that paid him an additional ten per cent of any new business he produced over an estimated break even point. Within three years he was the most productive and highest paid employee in the company.

After years of investigating businesses I have found that duties, responsibilities, work environments, and stress requirements, for the same titled job positions at different companies even within the same industry, wildly deviate. The diversity is so great, that basing job pay on what other companies are doing should be only a small factor in consideration of salary for any position.

Employer Secret 88: Some employers are overpaying some employees and underpaying other employees and neither the employer nor employee might be aware.

Basing pay on any job candidate's salary history is severely flawed for both the employee and employer. Previous employers may have been underpaying or overpaying for many reasons and there is no way for most prospective employers or employees to know.

- The job candidate might have come up against weaker negotiators at his or her previous place of employment and was able to bargain for higher pay.
- The job candidate might have come up against stronger negotiators at his or her previous place of employment and was held to lower pay.

- The job candidate could have received raises that were not justified.
- The job candidate could have been denied raises for reasons that were not justified. (Most salaries are not based on position profitability, and neither are raises.)
- Previous employers could be mismanaged and over paying or under paying any or all employees.

Jobs are as diverse as companies themselves. Employers should know exactly what they can pay for any position. Again, don't settle for the pay you were getting on your last job. (Remember, salary history should remain just that, history.)

Basing compensation on what other companies are paying for specific jobs is also subject to the same flaws. However, collecting information from a variety of sources versus the pay history of any one person may somewhat reduce the margins of error.

Arm yourself with additional data. Find the average pay range being paid by companies of similar size for the position you are applying for. In addition, build your value to the prospective employer. I have been offered many jobs for more than the advertised pay range and I contribute this to my 'job selling skills.'

You can only negotiate your starting wages *once.*

Become familiar with the job position you are considering and negotiation methods discussed herein. After you start working, no matter how much different the job is from what you expected, you probably cannot go back to the negotiating table.

◆————————————◆

22. The Secret Negotiating Tactics You Must Know

When I have consulted for Human Resource Departments and businesses, in addition to performing or advising research for competitive salary scales for specific positions, I have conducted or suggested what I call a 'Position *Probability*' study (not to be confused with 'Position *Profitability*' from the previous chapter.)

Employers often believe the number of qualified candidates available for any position is the number of resumes they receive. This leaves too much up to chance. The type of advertising the employer is doing, the media, the season, the actual ad, and recruiting methods can all dramatically skew any deduction of the true number of candidates available at any time. Not everyone available has responded to the employer's ad.

I wanted a more accurate method to find the probable number of qualified candidates for specific positions in particular geographic areas. This information would tell me:

- The approximate number of candidates that should be responding to the employer's advertising.
- How long the employer should search for a candidate.
- When the employer should make changes to advertising.

- When the employer should be looking for other advertising media.
- When the employer should make changes to recruiting methods.
- How much the employer was going to have to pay an employee.

I did a 'position probability' study for an employer who wanted to hire wastewater treatment plant operators.
This is what I wanted to know:
- The position qualifications required by the employer.
- How many qualified wastewater treatment plant operators are in the United States?
- How many wastewater treatment plants are in the United States?
- How many qualified wastewater treatment plant operators are there within the geographic region of the employer?
- How many schools train wastewater treatment plant operators, where are these schools located, and how many graduates have there been each year for the past ten years?

From this study I estimated that there was less than ten qualified candidates within fifty miles of the employer. This was not many and the employer admitted that when they advertised locally they had received only three resumes. She told me they had typically paid a much higher than industry average wage even for entry-level positions. I learned that the only other advertising they had done was on their Internet site.

After some digging, I found a school that offered an associate degree in wastewater treatment plant operation only two hundred miles from the employer. I asked the employer if they knew about this. She said that the company used to seek graduates from the school but the oil companies began recruiting them and paid a considerably higher starting wage. She said now the school no longer offered this training.

I contacted the school and requested the number of graduates for each year for the last ten years. I then asked to speak with a school counselor. (School counselors are one of my secret information sources. They know what's going on, usually have time to talk, and are great people.)

The counselor told me the school had removed the wastewater treatment operator degree from the curriculum. She said that until eight years ago the majority of graduates had gone on to work in municipalities. Then several oil refineries in the area needed workers and desired the knowledge of these graduates. For several years they hired every graduate.

Now that was no longer the case. Three years previously the refineries had fallen on difficult times and acquisitions and mergers began spawning layoffs.

By finding the number of graduates the school produced during the five years the oil refineries had been hiring, and checking the number of employees the oil refineries had laid off, I estimated there was a concentration of forty to sixty available qualified candidates still in the vicinity of the school.

Upon my advice the employer advertised the open positions in the college's hometown newspaper. Within two weeks my client received forty-two resumes. She was able to save a considerable amount of money in salaries and did not have to pay any employee relocation expenses.

This information put the employer in a much stronger negotiating position. This is the kind of research many job candidates are up against and don't even know about.

As a job seeker you need to do some research to strengthen your negotiating position. Information works both ways! Find out what your prospective employers are up against and you'll have a better idea of what you're up against.

- How many resumes will they get?
- How many qualified candidates will they have?
- How much can you get them to pay?

Experiment with researching these questions for advertised positions in different fields. Then prepare for your job search. There is more information available to the average person today than there has ever been in the history of the world. Visit the websites for The Department of Labor, the census statistics, your local municipality, company profiles, and the myriad of salary information sources. You could even start at my website, www.employersecrets.com

Secrets From the Dark Side

The Negotiation Process as a Test

Employer Secret 79: For some employers, the negotiation process is a test.

Sam Wright, the Human Resource Director of a local municipality who also serves on the budget committee, prided himself on having employees and purchasing agents that wouldn't get pushed around. He was certain that this was the way to make vendors cave in and keep costs down.

I was contracted to examine his hiring costs and employee retention costs. Seems that there was an unusually high turnover for these city employees in desirable positions with above average benefits.

There had been seventeen openings in the last year in a department of thirty. When I asked the young lady in human resources to show me the last twelve months of job candidate records, she took me to a room with over four hundred files. I was certain that I had not communicated my request clearly. I told her I only wanted to see the files for candidates that had completed the interview process but had not been successful in negotiations.

"That's exactly what these are," she stated.

"Do you mean to tell me you processed, interviewed, and made offers to over four hundred employees for seventeen openings?"

"Yes. We interviewed approximately another three hundred that we did not make offers to," she replied.

Sam practiced such hard line negotiating tactics that few candidates made it through the gauntlet. In addition, the employees were made miserable by the tougher tactics he expected them to use on the job.

After some number crunching I returned with my findings to Mr. Wright. I determined that the cost of hiring and replacing employees was costing the city a whopping twenty per cent of the entire payroll budget.

Delay Tactic

Employer Secret 81: Employers use the delay tactic.

I consider the delay tactic a hardball practice when used by an employer in hiring negotiations. As most candidates are operating from a need mode, they become frustrated when put off or ignored.

Usually, an employer uses this tactic when there are other candidates still in the running for the same position. I have discovered some employers using the delay tactic with interesting motives of which you need to beware.

One company I know starts the delay tactic after the offer is made. After negotiations the hiring manager tells candidates that their negotiating skills were so good; he will need to get approval for such a high salary. He then invites them in to 'meet the gang.' This is by spending a day at the company while he awaits 'approval.'

The reason is this; people act differently when they believe they have the job. Their guard goes down. During this time, the candidate believes he or she is going to be one of the gang, and the employer observes the candidate with even more scrutiny.

Employer Secret 91: Employers make contingency offers as a delay tactic.

One employer offers every qualified candidate the job with a contingency. The candidate will need to take a few 'procedural tests.'

Candidates should use the delay tactic only for time to consider an offer. This delay period should not be more than forty-eight hours under normal circumstances.

Negotiation tactics can include conflict. If you have no real negotiating experience try practicing in less significant areas. Try making an offer next time you need services performed such as carpet cleaning or lawn mowing.

Bait and Switch

Employer Secret 82: Some employers practice bait and switch tactics.

CAUTION: Beware of this scenario:

The interviewer calls you to inform you that he has good news and bad news. The bad news: The position you applied for has been filled. The good news: He tells you there is a new opening and offers you the job. Of course the pay is less.

(How did less pay become part of the good news?)

Some employers never had the position you applied for available. Maybe they cannot afford to hire people of your caliber and this is how they attempt to get discount employees. Whatever the reason, this is a dishonest bait and switch tactic. I wouldn't want to depend on people like this for my livelihood.

How Getting What You Want Might Keep You From Getting What You Need

Employer Secret 83: Some employers go for your heart.

Mr. Myer, a technology company President, hired me to perform an appraisal on a similar business that he was considering purchasing. An appraisal requires complete access to all company files and records. The subject company owner, Mr. Tower, was at first understandably apprehensive though he was motivated to sell his business to my client. I had just completed an appraisal on my client's company.

During the normal course of data gathering and review, I found that the employees of Mr. Tower's company, while all with similar education, experience, certifications, and seniority, were being paid considerably less than Mr. Myer's employees.

Although not competing for the same customers, both companies were in the same market within one hundred miles of each other.

Due to the nature of the businesses and the time needed to inspect records, I spent enough time at the physical location of each company to see that the morale at Mr. Tower's business was much the same as Mr. Myer's company.

When I questioned Mr. Tower about his pay scales he informed me that he had a 'crackerjack' HR manager, Don, and left all employee decisions up to him. As I my appraisal would be a factor in my client's acquisition decision, I performed an in depth interview with key management employees.

During my meeting with Don I learned that he had risen from salesperson to sales manager before taking over Human Resources. During his seven years of employment he had brought the closely held company from the verge of bankruptcy to a healthy annual profit growth each year.

When I hinted about the light salaries he leaned back in his chair and crossed his arms sending a reluctant signal. He excused himself and came back with his boss, Mr. Myer.

"Don has some concern about revealing what he feels is proprietary information. I have assured him that you and your client Mr. Tower, are under strict confidentiality agreements and have given him the green light to answer all of your questions," stated Mr. Myer.

With that Don resumed his position behind his desk and a slight grin appeared on his face as he started, "Well, my father taught me a negotiating technique long ago that has enabled me to sell for more and hire for less."

As I anticipated the unveiling, he told me this story.

"My father ran a car dealership all of his life. I was at his side before I could walk and have pictures of myself sleeping in the backseat of cars in the showroom when I was a baby. He sold numerous families every car they ever bought. He received many sales awards and seldom did I hear him have to reduce a price. He always told me to "find out what makes everyone tick." He said "it's never money makes a heart beat."

"That's a fine story, Don. But how does this apply to your employees?" I asked.

"Well whenever I decide on a new hire, before I begin any negotiations, I go to work finding out what makes their heart beat. If I haven't hit the button I'll schedule a third interview. I guess you could call it a heart to heart.

My father would find out what made his customers tick and go to work. He knew Mr. Todd, the banker, had a big ego. So every time Mr. Todd bought a car my dad placed "Congratulations Mr. Todd on Your New Cadillac" on our lighted sign in front of the dealership for two weeks.

Our neighbor, Mrs. Davis, lived for her grandchildren who she cared for after school. Even though she drove a seven year-old car, anytime it when in the shop, Dad made sure she had a new minivan to drive. You can bet where everyone of her kids and those grandkids bought their cars."

"So you give your employees minivans and put their names in lights?' I queried with a grin.

"Close. I focus on a candidate's motivational button. If it is recognition, I create a title, paint their name on a parking space, and include them in our PR articles. If I find out they live for sports, I might include season baseball tickets. Once I hit that button and concentrate there, money always becomes secondary."

"Don, aren't most people really motivated by money?"

"My Dad said no. He said that money was only the means to fund a person's true motivation. If a candidate or employee thinks money is their number one motivation, I don't argue, I look for what they think is the secondary motivator, and I focus there. Even when a person believes money is first in and of itself, second can be a very strong position."

I must say that Don's creativity was commendable and he had mastered learning about his job candidates and customers. Since that day I have met several employers that practice similar techniques, some more sophisticated with a complex severance package, bonus plan, relocation package, insurance benefits, stock option, vacation time, and car or car allowance, to name a few.

What's important to you when entering a negotiation for your livelihood is to know what your motivation is. One great question I've asked that helps people understand themselves better is: *What do you spend your money on?*

You should know what your true motivations are. Go beyond the money. The last thing you want is for someone on the opposite side of any negotiation table to find your hidden or underlying motivators before you do.

I have known people who collected bank vaults of money and are still unhappy. Many times this is because they became so entrenched in the process of collecting the money they lost sight of their true motivations. If they are lucky enough to rediscover them, they are often too late.

Employer Secret 84: Some employers practice this tactic of negotiation: *When the negotiation issue is money, talk exhaustively about any other issue except money.*

Employers have an abundance of negotiating currency including:

- car allowances
- expense accounts
- disability
- bonuses
- stock options
- profit sharing
- vacation and paid sick days
- retirement plans
- commission
- overtime
- relocation expenses

Insurance
- dental
- health
- vision
- life

There are certainly some perks, benefits, and bonuses that are worth obtaining. Sometimes these items can become creative deal commodities when an employer faces salary budget restrictions.

This is the point; People are motivated by egotistical rewards, greed, emotional requirements, and acceptance, and can sometimes be manipulated into selling themselves monetarily short in the negotiation process. Don't become so distracted or confused by negotiation items that you lose sight of your objectives. Your employer will be served the best when you are happy and motivated. *Negotiate for the package that will make you want to give the employer your best.*

Once you know the *pay range,* if you want to know where you stand, negotiate every other item first before money. As the value, cost, and complexity of employee benefits has changed, you need to know what they are offering. What health insurance coverage, stock option plan, and retirement plan is being offered?

Nowadays these values alone can be worth as much as the salary. There are companies on the Internet that for a fee, will evaluate any job offer for you.

Section V Summary

Most of us are familiar with the old standard sayings or laws of negotiation. These old sayings do not all work for job negotiation. Job negotiation is different.

Business is about profit. *It makes no difference how much someone is paid if they produce acceptably more profit than expense (and they can prove it.)*

Know the worth of the position.
Learn the 'Position Profitability'

Beware of employer secret negotiating tactics.

The Seven New Laws Of Job Negotiation

Old Law: Everything is negotiable.
New Law One: *Your performance is not negotiable.*

Old Law: Whoever mentions a number first loses.
New Law Two: *Whoever mentions a number first chooses.*

Old Law: The strongest negotiation tool is the ability to walk away from the table.
New Law Three: *Before you walk away from their table, make sure you have food on your table.*

Old Law: Look out for number one.

New Law Four: *If you consider yourself number one, look out.*

Old Law: Don't leave money on the table.

New Law Five: *Don't put your money on the table.*

Old Law: Drive a hard bargain.

New Law Six: Don't be hard to bargain with.

Old Law: Never let them see you sweat.

New Law Seven: *Let them know that once you're hired, you'll work up a sweat.*

▼▼▼▼▼▼▼▼▼▼▼▼▼▼▼▼▼▼▼▼▼▼▼▼▼▼▼▼▼▼▼`

Now Get That Job!

I have used every principle in this book to get everything I want. Now you can use these same methods and ideas too.

The following activities will help you and you have my permission to write them as shown for personal use:

1. Make a 3x5 or 4x6 card with the principles of LEAP and on the back write :

   You are the service or product.
   The employer is the customer.
   You are selling.
   The employer is buying.

2. Then get a second card and write:
   'The Seven A's of Persuasion'
   Announce, Arouse, Align, Affirm,
   Assure, Assist, Adjourn

Then include:

'Three Steps to Effective Empathy'

STEP ONE
*First, you must determine if the other person
has a need or desire.*

STEP TWO
*Secondly, you must see the other person's
need or desire from his or her perspective or best interests.*
THIS IS INFORMED EMPATHY.
THIS IS CRITICAL.

STEP THREE
*Third, you need to relate their need or desire with the
closest need or desire of your own in order to invoke the
same or similar feelings within yourself.*

On the back write: Fly Your Flag!

F   First Words

L   Listening Ability

A   Attitude and Appearance

G   Genuineness (in your voice and body
     language)

Become *likeable* by being *'able to like.'*

3. Get a third card for:

Learn *who* your employer is.
Learn your employer's needs and desires.
Use the 'Nine Lessons of Listening Science'
Lessons One, Two, and Three
Shut up
Listening Science Lesson Four
Ask Questions
Listening Science Lesson Five
Ask pertinent questions.
Listening Science Lesson Six
Relate to Them
Listening Science Lesson Seven
Be Interested
Listening Science Lesson Eight
Remember What They've Said
Listening Science Lesson Nine
Timing is critical.

on the back write:

The Seven New Laws Of Job Negotiation

New Law One: *Your performance is not negotiable.*

New Law Two: Whoever mentions a number first *chooses*

New Law Three: Before you walk away from their table, *make sure you have food on your table.*

New Law Four: If you consider yourself number one, look out.

New Law Five: Don't put your money on the table.

New Law Six: Don't be hard to bargain with.

New Law Seven: Let them know that once you're hired, you'll work up a sweat.

Keep these cards where you will see them everyday.

4. Get your SELF together and keep it in a safe place. (See the end of this book for information on how to get a "SELF Kit.")

The summaries at the end of each section of this book cover the main points and are great to review. Take control of your career destiny by practicing the principles outlined in this book. Don't become one of the people who are *dissatisfied with their jobs within one year.*

Become aware.
Look around you and become inspired.
Inspiration is the first step of motivation.

For more information, job resources,
and books by Phil Baker
visit EMPLOYER SECRETS on the Internet at:
www.employersecrets.com

◆————————————◆

Index

Thank you.

About the Author

Phil Baker has spent years working with and consulting for business owners and corporate executives. He has owned or served on the board of dozens of companies. He has participated in the sale of hundreds of businesses while earning numerous sales and business awards.

Phil started the first successful fax/courier document service. He was an early developer of electronic advertising in 1983. In 1989 he co-founded the first pizza box advertising and printing company. Phil was the first to sell and ship pizza boxes to East Germany when the wall came down.

Phil is the innovator of 'FLAG,' 'LEAP,' 'SELF,' "The Three Principle Steps to Effective Empathy,' 'The Seven A's of Persuasion,' 'The Nine Lessons of Listening Science,' 'The Greatest Job Hunting Principle,' 'The Three Types of Assurance Statements,' and 'The Seven New Laws of Job Negotiation,' all described in this book.

In his years of experience as a Business Broker, Appraiser, business owner, HR Director, salesperson, consultant, and entrepreneur, Phil realized the growing gap between employers and job candidates and saw the need to better inform job candidates of the employers' situation and hiring practices. As the legal responsibilities of the employer have increased to encompass all facets of the hiring process, employers have innovated new processes and policies that directly affect the job candidate.

Phil Baker wrote this book to help job hunters better understand the hiring process and be greater prepared. Now he reveals to you secret employer hiring practices to help you get the job and pay you want.

To inquire about this book in any other format such as audio please contact:

DreamCatcher Publishing, Inc.
Telephone: 314 972-1505
Fax: 314 972-8448
Email: orders@employersecrets.com

Mailing Address:
DreamCatcher Publishing
1050 St. Francois
Flosissant, MO 63031

Quick Order Form for this book:
Employer Secrets

Internet Orders: www.employersecrets.com

Telephone Orders: 314 972-1505

Fax orders: 314 972-8448

Email Orders: orders@employersecrets.com

Postal Orders: DreamCatcher Publishing
 1050 St. Francois
 Flosissant, MO 63031

Name_____

Address _____

City _____ State _____ Zip_____

Telephone _____

email address _____

Please send me _____ copies of Employer Secrets at $16.95 each. Please add $ 5.00 per copy for shipping in USA.

Missouri residents add 7% sales tax.

Total $ _____   Check ☐   Money Order ☐

Visa ☐   Mastercard ☐   Discover ☐

Card Number_____

Name on Card_____Exp. Date_____

Prices subject to change without notice.

DreamCatcher Publishing, Inc.
1050 St. Francois
Flosissant, MO 63031

Quick Order Form for this book:
Employer Secrets

Internet Orders: www.employersecrets.com

Telephone Orders: 314 972-1505

Fax orders: 314 972-8448

Email Orders: orders@employersecrets.com

Postal Orders: DreamCatcher Publishing
                  1050 St. Francois
                  Flosissant, MO 63031

Name_____

Address _____

City _____ State _____ Zip_____

Telephone _____

email address _____

Please send me _____ copies of Employer Secrets at $16.95 each. Please add $ 5.00 per copy for shipping in USA.

Missouri residents add 7% sales tax.

Total $ _____   Check ☐   Money Order ☐

Visa ☐   Mastercard ☐   Discover ☐

Card Number_____

Name on Card_____ Exp. Date_____

Prices subject to change without notice.